MANKIND AT THE TURNING POINT

MANKIND
AT THE
TURNING POINT

Mihajlo Mesarovic and Eduard Pestel

The Second Report
to The Club of Rome

E. P. Dutton & Co., Inc. / Reader's Digest Press
New York 1974

To Future Generations

Published simultaneously in Canada by Clarke, Irwin & Company
Limited, Toronto and Vancouver

ISBN: 0-525-15230-X (cloth)
ISBN: 0-525-03945-7 (paper)

Library of Congress Catalog Card Number: 74-16787

CONTENTS

Contents

PREFACE

Many recent analyses of the long-term prospects for mankind have produced gloomy conclusions. Promptly, they were called doomsday prophecies. Yet the rapid succession of crises which are currently engulfing the entire globe are the clearest indication that humanity is at a turning point in its historical evolution. And the way to make doomsday prophecies self-fulfilling is to ignore the obvious signs of perils that lie ahead—which indeed are already felt—and rely solely on "faith." *Our scientifically conducted analysis of the long-term world development based on all available data points out quite clearly that such a passive course leads to disaster.* It is *most urgent* that we do not avert our eyes from the dangers ahead, but face the challenge squarely and assess alternative paths of development in a positive and hopeful spirit. Starting early enough on a new path of development can save mankind from traumatic experiences if not from catastrophes. The concept of the "organic growth" of mankind, as we have proposed in this report, is intended as a contribution toward achieving that end. Were mankind to embark on a path of organic growth, the world would emerge as a system of interdependent and harmonious parts, each making its own unique contribution, be it in economics, resources, or culture.

The concept of the organic growth of the world system is not to be construed as a simplistic one-world "monolithic" concept of world development; indeed a homogeneous one-world concept is essentially incompatible with a truly global approach to better the predicament of mankind. Such an approach must start from and preserve the world's regional diversity. Paths of development, region-specific rather than based on narrow national interests, must be designed to lead to a sustainable balance between the interdependent world-regions and to global harmony—that is, to mankind's growth as an "organic entity" from its present barely embryonic state.

The conclusions and recommendations reported in this book are derived from the analysis of alternative patterns of long-term world development using a flexible computer-based planning instrument which contains a multilevel regionalized model of the world system. The model is fundamentally different from any previously developed, for it recognizes the diversity that exists in the world, which is deeply rooted in the past, and which will undoubtedly prevail in the future; the model also represents the world as a system—that is, as a collection of mutually interacting and interdependent parts. The model is based on available data and understanding of the developmental processes in all relevant scientific disciplines. It also reflects the adaptive nature and subjective character intrinsic to any system involving human elements.

Several critical problem areas have been investigated, in particular the world food shortage, energy crises, population growth, and disparity in economic development. Two gaps, steadily widening, appear to be at the heart of mankind's present crises: the gap between man and nature, and the gap between "North" and "South," rich and poor. Both gaps must be narrowed if world-shattering catastrophes are to be avoided; but they can be narrowed only if global "unity" and Earth's "finiteness" are explicitly recognized.

The scientific foundation for the research, the findings of which this report attempts to communicate to the general public, was laid nearly three years ago, when the authors decided to develop a project concerned with the analysis of global issues which would realistically take into account the diversity of the many different world regions and would deal with issues concretely, rather than in abstract terms. We hoped thus to furnish political and economic decision-makers in various parts of the world with a comprehensive global planning tool, which could help them to act in anticipation of the crises at our doorstep and of those that loom increasingly large in the distance, instead of reacting in the spirit of short-term pragmatism.

The project, generously supported by the Volkswagen Foundation, has been repeatedly exposed to the scrutiny of the scientific community, at two international economics symposia and, recently, at a week-long conference attended by more than one hundred scientists of various disciplines at the International Institute for Applied Systems Analysis (IIASA) in Laxenburg near Vienna, Austria. For the science-oriented reader nearly thirty reports on all aspects of the project are available upon request from IIASA. (See Appendix IV, Bibliography; hundreds of references and sources not quoted in this general report are also listed in the IIASA technical reports.)

The language of the general report to The Club of Rome, presented herewith, is simple rather than technical. It should be easily understood by the interested layman although every effort has been made to preserve the precision and accuracy of our scientific approach.

Our work, which represents the central project of The Club of Rome's present activities, by no means terminates with the publication of this report and the scientific and technical reports referred to above. However, we believe that our findings and the general insights gained through intense preoccupation with the model, its data base, and the pressing issues of our time, not only amply justify this publication, but even compel us to focus the attention of the public at large on the urgent problems that lie ahead. Had we failed to do so, we would have violated one of our basic premises and committed the same fatal mistake repeatedly committed by too many decision-making processes: constructive action would be delayed rather than being undertaken in anticipation of critical future developments.

We strongly resent the suggestion, frequently made, that scientists should not publish statements and recommendations regarding situations in which there are elements of judgment or uncertainty and for which "scientific tests" cannot be conducted. This would effectively eliminate scientists from any consideration and discussion of mankind's long-term future, where such a degree of certainty is just not attainable. Scientists could thus be unduly penalized and forced to leave the arena of public discussion to those who have even less information about the world's future course. This does not imply that we actually question the intuition, experience, and wisdom of non-scientists. Rather, we hope that the frank and undisguised exposition of our views of the world will encourage fruitful discussion and cooperation with all those who are daily confronted with painful decisions in political and economic life.

In this spirit a number of meetings are already planned with public figures, political leaders from different parts of the world, and members and guests at The Club of Rome's 1974 plenary session on the "North-South" gap in Berlin, Germany. A seminar in April 1974 at the Woodrow Wilson International Center for Scholars, Washington, D.C., was attended by about seventy public figures. A similar meeting was held at "Haus Rissen" in Hamburg, Germany. Some leading technologists will meet at the International Institute for the Management of Technology (IIMT) in Milan, Italy, to consider important technological problems that will arise from the development of the vast regions that have yet to fully industrialize and that possibly will do so quite differently than the already industrialized areas have done.

Finally, we want to comment on certain omissions in this report. There will be hardly any mention of some crucial political problems resulting from increased military and ideological polarizations. This should not be construed as failure on our part to recognize the seriousness of such threats to the world community. Indeed, there is obviously no more effective short-cut to the destruction of mankind than an atomic war involving the superpowers and their respective military blocs. Even barring such an event, we are convinced that the continuous escalation of armament in an effort to maintain the balance of power is steadily decreasing the stability of other equally delicate world balances. Political and ideological confrontation are hardly new problems. The present novelty derives from the vast scale of the problems which is a result of the enormous economic power of the nations involved and particularly of the fantastic advance in destructive technology. We must therefore find a way to reduce modern armaments in order to remove the sword of Damocles hanging over the heads of all of us.

On the other hand, while this is an obvious and unquestionable prerequisite for lasting peace, there is a much more subtle and completely novel threat to man's survival that looms, every year more menacingly, beside that of an atomic holocaust: the cluster of worldwide problems—not only material in nature—growing at an incredible speed when viewed in historical perspective, and called by The Club of Rome the *"problématique humaine."* In fact, we believe that even without an atomic world war, human existence as we know it is threatened if no way can be found to resolve this crisis syndrome. Therefore we have concentrated our efforts in this report on a number of vital worldwide issues whose mastery we consider essential for man's survival and for an eventual transition into sustainable material and spiritual development of humanity. We believe that unless the issues treated in this book are mastered, there will be no disarmament of spirit and arms, and the disparities in the world will eventually drive mankind over the brink into final destruction.

To all our many collaborators and consultants (see Appendix I) we should like to extend our deep thanks for their

often decisive contributions to the research that is the back-
bone of this report. For the content of this report the
authors assume sole responsibility, realizing that the views
expressed are not necessarily shared by all our collaborators
and consultants.

Mihajlo Mesarovic   Eduard Pestel
Cleveland, Ohio   Hannover, Germany
August 1974

CHAPTER 1

Prologue: From Undifferentiated to Organic Growth

The World Has Cancer
and the Cancer Is Man.
A. Gregg *

Suddenly—virtually overnight when measured on a historical scale—mankind finds itself confronted by a multitude of unprecedented crises: the population crisis, the environmental crisis, the world food crisis, the energy crisis, the raw material crisis, to name just a few. New crises appear while the old ones linger on with the effects spreading to every corner of the Earth until they appear in point of fact as global, worldwide, crises. Attempts at solving any one of these in isolation has proven to be temporary and at the expense of others; to ease the shortage of energy or raw materials by measures which worsen the condition of the environment means, actually, to solve nothing at all. Real solutions are apparently interdependent; collectively, the

---

* A. Gregg,"A Medical Aspect of the Population Problem," *Science* 121 (1955), 681.

whole multitude of crises appears to constitute a single global crisis-syndrome of world development.

The intensity of the crisis in global world development and the elusiveness of effective measures to bring about a solution challenge premises that have long been most fundamental in guiding the evolution of human society. Although these premises have paved the way for human progress in the past, they have also, finally, led to the present conditions. Mankind, therefore, appears to be at a turning point: to continue on the old road—that is, to follow the traditional route, unchallenged, into the future—or to start on a new path. In the search for such a new direction the old premises must be re-evaluated.

One such premise concerns the phenomenon of growth. Many of the global crises have been attributed to continuous and rapid growth. It has been argued, therefore, that growth must be stopped—or at the very least, deliberately retarded. Conversely, it has also been maintained that solutions of the world crises could be found only through continued growth. The fact is that both of these points of view require a great deal of qualification and more explicit definition before either one can be accepted as correct on a rational—rather than an ideological or emotional—basis. In other words, we need to know what is meant by "growth," and in what sense that growth is considered as desirable or undesirable. Growth, after all, is a process, not an object; it cannot be pointed at physically, like a chair or table, for the sake of explication; rather, it must be conceptually defined.

But defining growth (especially in support of positions "for" or "against" growth) is not necessarily straightforward —as the confusion characteristic of current debate on growth or no-growth indicates. On certain growth issues there would seem to exist universal agreement. Consider, for example, the issue of population growth. Few would quarrel with the position that the global population cannot and should not be permitted to grow unchecked forever. That the population must level off some time, i.e., that population *growth should stop,* is the view gaining universal acceptance. On the other hand, none would argue against the growth in medical services leading to increased life expectancy and declining mortality rates; but this leads to increase rather than decline in population. The area of material consumption provides yet another example of the complexity of the growth issue and highlights the peril in taking a stand for or against growth as an abstract concept. It is a well-established fact that in the world's developed, industrialized regions materials consumption has reached proportions of preposterous waste. In those regions there must now be a relative decline in the use of various materials. On the other hand, in some other less fully developed world regions, there must be substantial growth in the use of some essential commodities, either for food production or for industrial production. The very existence of the population in those regions depends on such growth. Hence, unqualified arguments "for" or "against" growth are naive; *to grow or not to grow is neither a well-defined nor a relevant question until the location, sense, and subject of growing and the growth process itself are defined.*

To appreciate how rich and varied the concept of growth is one has to recall the growth processes as found in Nature. (See Brief on Growth.) Two types of growth processes are of interest here: one is *undifferentiated growth,* the other is *organic growth,* or growth with differentiation. In the undifferentiated type, growth occurs through replication of cells by cell division: one cell divides into two, two into four, four into eight, and so on until, very rapidly, there are millions and billions of cells. For example, if the doubling time is one hour, the first cell will have become nearly 17 million cells after twenty-four hours, while after forty-eight hours there would be more than 280 trillion (280,000,000,000,000) cells. In undifferentiated growth all of the new cells are replicas of the first; growth is in quantity only. The result is a purely exponential increase of the cells' numbers. Organic growth, in contrast, involves a process of differentiation, which means that various groups of cells begin to differ in structure and function. The cells become organ-specific according to the developmental process of the organism: liver cells become distinct from brain cells; brain cells are differentiated from the bone cells, etc. During and after differentiation, the number of cells can still increase, and the organs grow in size; but while some organs grow, others might decline.*

The current discussion on the crisis in world development centers on growth as though it were necessarily the undifferentiated type.† There is no reason, however, why parallels to organic growth should not be drawn upon: indeed, our analysis reported in this book, of the options available to mankind for dealing with the world crisis-syn-

---

* The equilibrium reached in organic growth is dynamic, not static. This is so because in a mature living organism, the body is constantly being renovated. A human body, for example, renovates itself approximately every seven years.

† H. Cole et al., *Thinking About the Future: A Critique of The Limits to Growth* (Chatto & Windus, Sussex University Press, 1973).

drome, points out the crucial importance of the organic growth concept for the future development of mankind.

The analogy between the organic growth of an organism and that of the world system is, of course, only an analogy. It refers to the specialization of various parts of an organic system and to the functional interdependence between its constituent parts in the sense that none of them is self-contained but rather each has to fulfill a role assigned through historical evolution. However, the analogy shows vividly the immensity of change in magnitude and in kind which is needed for mankind to start on a new course of global world development.

In the past the world community was merely a collection of fundamentally independent parts. Under such conditions each of the parts could grow—for better or worse—as it pleased. In the new conditions, exemplified by the global crises-syndrome, the world community has been transformed into a world system, i.e., a collection of functionally interdependent parts. Each part—whether a region or a group of nations—has its own contribution to make to the organic development of mankind: resources, technology, economic potential, culture, etc. In such a system the growth of any one part depends on the growth or non-growth of others. Hence the undesirable growth of any one part threatens not only that part but the whole as well. If the world system could embark on the path of organic growth, however, the organic interrelationships would act as a check against undifferentiated growth anywhere in the system.

If the concept of growth were restricted solely to undifferentiated growth, there would be no question but that the growth process—practically *all* growth processes—would have to stop. One does not need any complicated analysis to arrive at that conclusion. It is easy to see why. If, for example, an economy grows at a 5 percent annual rate, it would, by the end of the next century, reach a level more than 500 times greater (or 50,000 percent higher) than the current level. Even if the use of materials were to decline sharply in relation to the rise in economic output, the problems of acquiring, processing, and disposing of the materials would be staggering. Even the leaders of growth-oriented enterprises realize this. As the former board chairman of a major U.S. bank has written recently: "It has become popular to speak of the energy crisis as only the tip of the iceberg, and indeed it is. But those who use that figure of speech are usually referring to the shortage of other things (plastics, for example) because plants have not been built to meet the booming worldwide demand. That is not the real problem: the real problem is that all those shortages combined are truly the tip of a much larger, much more profound iceberg. Under the surface of the waters we are sailing is the cold hard fact that we are using up irreplaceable resources at a rate that simply cannot be sustained. Building more plants to use them up faster is not the answer. So the energy crisis provides us with a dress rehearsal—the trial run of a drama that we must someday see enacted on a much larger stage." * Growth for growth's sake in the sense of ever increasing numbers and larger size simply cannot continue forever.

On the basis of that irrefutable diagnosis, a prescription of no-growth administered immediately and worldwide might seem to be indicated. And, indeed, such a prescription might serve admirably—*if* the world were a uniform entity, which

* *Los Angeles Times,* December 1973.

it is not; and *if* the world could be counted on to evolve into a uniform, one-world entity, which cannot and ought not to happen; and *if* growth and development could be measured along a single dimension for the entire world, which cannot be done. In fact growth occurs at varying rates along different paths in different parts of the world. While undifferentiated growth is assuming truly cancerous qualities in some parts of the world, the very existence of man is threatened daily in some other part by lack of growth; e.g., in regional food production.

It is this pattern of unbalanced and undifferentiated growth which is at the heart of the most urgent problems facing humanity—and a path which leads to a solution is that of organic growth.

In Nature organic growth proceeds according to a "master plan," a "blueprint." According to this master plan diversification among cells is determined by the requirements of the various organs; the size and shape of the organs and, therefore, their growth processes are determined by their function, which in turn depends on the needs of the whole organism.

Such a "master plan" is missing from the processes of growth and development of the world system. The master plan that regulates the growth of an organism has evolved through the process of natural selection; it is encoded in the genes and is given from the start to the growing organism, so that development of the organism is specified by it; the plan and the organism are inseparable. But the organic growth of mankind is *not* inherent in the present trend of world development. There is nothing to suggest that the transition from undifferentiated to organic growth will result from the present direction of development. Nor can it

Brief on Growth

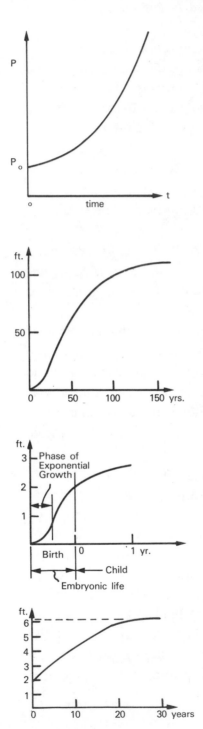

Figure A Exponential Growth

Exponential growth takes place in many commonplace situations, e.g., when savings grow with a constant rate of compound interest, or when population grows with birth rate larger than the death rate. Here the concept of "doubling time" is important. This is the period of time in which the population doubles. For example, at a 7 percent annual growth rate the doubling time is about 10 years. In general, if the constant annual growth rate is equal to g, then the doubling time in years is, with rather good approximation, equal to 70/g.

Figure B Growth of an Oak Tree

In contrast to mammals, such as man, plants grow throughout their lifetimes. However, towards the end of their lives their growth rate decreases. An oak tree, even after a lifetime of 150 years, grows about 3 inches per year. In the beginning, as with a human embryo, plant growth appears to be exponential. But after having achieved a certain critical living mass, this phase is over, and organic-"tapered"-growth sets in.

Figure C Logistic Growth

In many instances, growth is very rapid at first, but it tapers off as time progresses. This is the case, for example, for growth of almost all animals. In the embryonic stages, growth is rapid, and there is little structure to the embryo. But in the original cell there is a master plan which controls the organism's growth. As the structure increases in its complexity, the pattern of growth becomes different, slower — and in mammals even ceases — as the organism reaches its full adult complexity.

Figure D Growth of Human

Mammals, including man, grow in their childhood and youth, after which they stop growing. In no phase of normal development does exponential, undifferentiated, growth take place.

be assumed that such a plan will be injected by a *deus ex machina*. The master plan has yet to evolve through the exercise of options by the people who constitute the world system. To this extent *the options facing humanity contain the genesis of an organic growth*. And it is in this sense that mankind is at a turning point in its history: to continue along the path of cancerous undifferentiated growth or to start on the path of organic growth.

The transition from the present undifferentiated and unbalanced world growth to organic growth will lead to the creation of a new mankind. Such a transition would represent a dawn, not a doom, a beginning, not the end. Will mankind have the wisdom and will power to evolve a sound strategy to achieve that transition? In view of historical precedents, one might, legitimately, have serious doubts— *unless the transition evolves out of necessity. And this is where the current and future crises—in energy, food, materials, and the rest—can become error-detectors, catalysts for change, and as such blessings in disguise. The solutions of these crises will determine on which of the two paths mankind has chosen to travel.*

CHAPTER 2

Nature of Global Crises

Crises are not new to human society. In fact, mankind has never been crisis-free for any substantial period of time. And history shows that sooner or later man has always been able to overcome the crises of his day. In retrospect it seems that all crises in modern times were solved soon enough to prevent a reversal of the triumphant march of progress.

Is there any reason to believe that the crises of our era will not be resolved as successfully as the crises of the past were resolved? Is there any reason why we should not go about our business as usual, confident that the precedents of the past will apply to the future, and that all our crises will be taken care of in due time?

The answer to these questions is yes, there is ample reason to believe that the problems of our time will *not* be solved in the routine course of events. For one thing, the numerous crises of the present exist simultaneously and with a strongly woven interrelationship between them. We do not have the luxury of dealing with one crisis at a time. Furthermore, the scale and global character of the present crises differ from the nature and scale of most past crises. The most important factor, however, that separates the current series of crises from the crises of the past is the character of their causes. In the past, major crises had *negative* origins: they were caused by the evil intentions of aggressive rulers or governments, or by natural disasters regarded as evil according to human values—plagues, floods, earthquakes, and so on. In contrast, many of the crises of the present have *positive* origins: they are consequences of actions that were, at their genesis, stimulated by man's best intentions. To reduce human labor by exploiting the non-human energy sources in Nature, for example, was a goal no one quarreled with but it led to the present energy crises. Strenthening of the group—be it the family, community, or nation—by having a large number of children was commendable; but it led to the population crises. To reduce human suffering and prolong human life by conquering disease was certainly a noble aim; but it led to a substantial increase in the population. Large construction projects, such as building roads, dams and canals, agriculture and forestry practices, hunting and breeding of animals, mining and industrial engineering, etc.—in other words the imposition of man's design on the natural environment for man's own good—was man's way of "taming" Nature; but it led to the environmental crises. Today it seems that the basic values, which are ingrained in human societies of all ideologies and religious persuasions, are ultimately responsible for many of our troubles. But if future crises are to be avoided, how then should these values be readjusted?

Should traditional "good" become revisionist "bad"? Is it necessary to abandon the values which have, so far, served man so well, as evidenced by his continuous progress?

In the last three centuries, human progress can be measured in terms of man's triumphs over Nature. Our successes have been so great that man's supremacy over Nature has been taken for granted: Nature has not yet been defeated, but it certainly has appeared to be in irreversible retreat. Where Nature has still held out, man has considered his ultimate control simply a question of time. The "war on cancer," for example, was not really launched as a war—for a war is a struggle that may be lost—but as an expedition to liquidate the remnants of an enemy who may hold out for a while, but whose ultimate defeat was assumed to be inevitable. In the new crises, however, there is evidence that the adversary is Nature once again, an adversary who is not at all beaten, and who is in some ways more elusive and more formidable than we ever imagined.

Consider, for example, our attitude toward natural resources. In an unrestrained pursuit of economic and material growth, we have put faith in the presumably inexhaustible supply of natural resources: food, energy, raw materials, etc. But now we have discovered that these essential resources are by no means infinitely available. Even if we accept as plausible that substitutions will be found as the supply of presently essential resources dwindles, we can by no means be certain that the substitutions will be found exactly when they are needed and in the precise quantity that is needed. Given this uncertainty, we cannot be sure that progress will continue uninterrupted. And considering the complexity of the systems that govern the course of human society, any interruption is bound to have serious, and perhaps disastrous, consequences.

Man's dependency on Nature goes very deep indeed; his use and misuse of resources is only part of the picture. As man has become the dominant force in the shaping of life-systems on the Earth, his ascent has been accompanied by a reduction of the biological diversity in Nature. Species not perceived to be in the service of man have been systematically reduced in number or eliminated. Should this trend continue, Earth will soon be inhabited by a diminished number of species. Today we understand much better than our ancestors that the existence of all life on Earth—our own included—depends on the stability of the ecological system. An Earth with less diverse inhabitants might not continue to possess the stability essential for adaptation and survival. And if our ecosystem breaks down—even if only temporarily—the effect on mankind will be calamitous. The ultimate irony confronting technological man may well reside in the fact that Nature's most potent threats to human welfare are not her destructive power—earthquakes, tornadoes and hurricanes—but the fragility of the web of life, the delicacy of those skeins which bind species to species and which comprise the dynamic bonds which relate the animate and inanimate realms so inextricably in the processes of life.

BRIEF ON MAN'S INTERFERENCE IN NATURE

Being "but a part of nature," man has always affected and has always been affected by his environment. However, due to the disproportionate increase in numbers and due to increased sophistication of man's intervention in natural processes, the interference of man is taking on a completely new dimension with unpredictable and potentially

*catastrophic consequences; this is beginning to cause con-
cern from an unsuspected source: the scientists who origi-
nated and developed such techniques of intervention. A
good example is the most recent appeal by a group of
microbiologists to the world scientific community at large
to refrain from conducting the experiments that involve in-
serting into bacteria the genes which are resistant to anti-
biotics or the genes of viruses. The potential danger to
which the appeal specifically addresses itself is due to the
fact that the bacteria often used in scientific experiments
of this kind is a common inhabitant in the human intestine.
A prospect of such a resistant bacteria escaping and infect-
ing the population must be taken into account; it implies
the possibility of loosing new plagues upon the world. The
event was properly hailed by the scientists themselves as
a historical landmark of restraint to conduct experiments
purely for the sake of scientific curiosity. It represents a
reversal of the cherished tradition that nothing should interfere with the sciences' search for truth. However, even if
the experiments in which new, resistant bacteria are created
are foolproof, there exists a real danger in: (1) the potential
of using such a new technique for biological warfare; (2)
the possibility of such experiments being conducted outside
of a properly controlled laboratory. Although the use of this
less-than-a-year-old technique is still in the hands of experts, it will be a "high school project within a few years." **
The solemn high-level warnings against conducting such experiments whose consequences cannot be predicted could
hardly be considered as a sufficient deterrent then. But
there are many others, even if considered less spectacular,
examples of unknown and potentially harmful consequences
of man's intervention in nature.*

When man imposes his own design on Nature, he inter-
feres with the process of natural selection. The consequences of such interventions cannot be predicted. In his
pursuit of short-term gains, man is introducing into the
ecosystem a large number of inadequately tested new chem-
icals, which may have serious and widespread biological
implications. Countless living organisms could be affected,
including man himself. In the interest of his own comfort in

---

* Paul Berg et al., "Potential Biohazards of Recombinant DNA Molecules,"
Science, Vol. 5, No. 4148, July 1974.

the present, and in the name of progress, man may thus degrade the quality of his own species in the future.

The ever-widening gap between man and Nature—his physical isolation and his mental estrangement from Nature —is the logical consequence of the traditional concept of progress; for progress in world development has led increasingly to a process of undifferentiated growth, based on man's erroneous assumption that Nature's supporting system was inexhaustible in every respect. The modern crises are, in fact, man-made, and differ from many of their predecessors in that they *can* be dealt with. The choices are complicated, but they exist. Obviously, we cannot clean up the air by turning off all the machinery (since that would instantly create other sorts of crises), but the fact is that modern man at least has that option, and that know-how. Medieval people had no choice but to allow the plague to run its course; they could not "turn off" disease-carrying rats.

If we are to deal effectively with the crises of the present, we must understand their origin and nature, their linkages and interactions. It is our intention in this book to analyze the crises in the world development in concrete rather than abstract terms; otherwise our analyses will be just another academic exercise, of which there is no shortage. Specifically, we shall ask the following questions:

1. Are the crises—energy, food, raw materials, etc.— persistent, or are they aberrations due, possibly, to oversight or neglect?

2. Can the crises be solved within local, national, or regional boundaries, or must truly lasting solutions be effected within a global framework?

3. Can the crises be solved by traditional measures which

have always been confined to an isolated aspect of social development, such as technology, economics, politics, etc. —or must the strategy for solution be more comprehensive, involving all aspects of social life simultaneously?

4. How urgent is the resolution of the crises? Will delay buy time and make the implementation of solutions less painful? Or are solutions made more elusive by delay?

5. Is there a way to solve the total crises by cooperation without undue sacrifice on the part of any of the constituents of the world system; or is there the danger that some could gain permanently by seeking confrontation with their partners in the global context?

Whenever one deals with the sort of problems and questions outlined above, a decision concerning the time-horizon of the study has to be made. Most of the so-called "long looks" into the future do not extend beyond the year 2000. If things seem manageable by then, everything is proclaimed satisfactory. Granted, the degree of uncertainty grows with each extension of time. But, as will be demonstrated time and again in this report, the dynamics of the world system require twenty years or more for the effects of change to be accurately measured and fully revealed. Moreover, the delays involved in the implementation of decisions can be formidable. To construct a power plant takes five to ten years from the decision to build a plant to its actual operation. And this length of time is merely the product of technological and administrative requirements; when basic human attitudes must change and social adjustments must be made, implementation takes much longer. Given these delays, a twenty-five-year period cannot accurately reveal the dynamics of the system: basic and important trends simply cannot be assessed within such a "short" time period.

What appears to be a minor deviation in a twenty-year assessment can become a major upset after forty years—that is, after the evolution has been subjected fully to the momentum of change. An example of the dynamics at work will be found in Chapter 9, in the analysis of the supply and demand for food. By the year 2000 the demand for food in South Asia will be about 30 percent greater than the supply—an alarming but conceivably a manageable gap. With advanced planning, the gap could be reduced to as low as 10 percent. However, if the same projections are extended another twenty-five years, the deficit rises to over 100 percent—clearly a catastrophic disparity.

The analyses in this book extend over a period of fifty years. If, during this coming half-century, a viable world system emerges, an organic growth pattern will have been established for mankind to follow thereafter. If a viable system does not develop, projections for the decades thereafter may be academic.

CHAPTER 3

Emerging World System

Change in the course of world development from undifferentiated to organic growth would have been a matter of
choice and good will rather than necessity if the world had
not evolved into a state in which nations and regions from
all over the globe not merely influence but strongly depend
on each other. Contributing to this transition, in addition to
the traditional political, ideological, and economic ties, are
new global world problems specific for our era such as
worldwide dependence on a common stock of raw materials,
problems in providing energy and food supply, sharing of
the common physical environment on land, sea, and air,
etc. The world community appears as a "system" by which
we mean collection of interdependent parts rather than
merely a group of largely independent entities as was the
case in the past. And as a consequence a disturbance of the
normal state of affairs in any part of the world quickly

spreads all over the world, as many recent events unmistakably show. Let us briefly trace the developments in such an event.

The winter 1971–72, with its prolonged low temperatures and strong icy winds all over Eastern Europe, effectively destroyed one third of the Russian winter wheat crop. Surprisingly, the government bureaucracy ignored the situation, and the spring wheat acreage allocation remained unchanged. Since the direct per-capita consumption of wheat in that region is rather high (three times higher than in North America), it was urgent that the deficit be eliminated. In July 1972 the U.S. government extended a $750 million credit to the Soviet Union for the purchase of grain over a three-year period. Actually, the value of the purchase increased significantly before the delivery got underway since food prices soared all over the world. The price of wheat doubled in North America—hitherto a bastion of cheap food supply. Public resentment arose because people felt that in effect they were being made to pay for a transaction that did not involve the ordinary citizen. More important, and much more unfortunately, that same year's late monsoon heavily damaged the crops on the Indian subcontinent, resulting in a disastrous loss in food supply, which came in the aftermath of a tragic war. Nowhere was wheat to be found, for most of the world's surplus had been sold. Then a drought hit China and Africa and while China was acquiring whatever foodstuffs were left on the market, hundreds of thousands of Africans faced starvation. In a similar situation several years earlier, millions of tons of wheat had been rushed from North America to avert disaster; but this time only two hundred thousand tons could be made available.

The most outstanding lesson which can be drawn from

these events is a realization of how strong the bonds among nations have become. A bureaucratic decision in one region, perhaps the action of just one individual—not to increase the spring wheat acreage—resulted in a housewives' strike against soaring food prices in another part of the world and in tragic suffering in yet another part of the world. If the world is already interdependent to that extent, and interdependence is certain to increase, should regional or national decisions still be made in isolation, in total ignorance of their effects on other parts of the world system?

The world cannot be viewed any more as a collection of some 150-odd nations and an assortment of political and economic blocs. Rather, the world must be viewed as consisting of nations and regions which form a world system through an assortment of interdependences.

However, such interdependence is not the only new feature of the emerging world system. A subtle and very fundamental transformation is taking place. In earlier eras of lesser complexity different cultural or economic aspects, including their effects on technical development and natural environment, could have been considered separately. Today, many of these phenomena have become interdependent which greatly complicates any search for the solution of various critical problems. Traditionally, in order to understand what appeared to him to be diverse aspects of reality, man has developed different scientific disciplines: physics, chemistry, biology, technology, economics, the social and political sciences, philosophy, ethics, theology, etc. And in solving different problems man has relied on experience and expertise in relevant disciplines. But today's problems require knowledge from a number of, if not all, disciplines. For example, the solution of the world food supply crisis is a question not just of agronomy and economics, but of ecology, the physical and social sciences, and many others. How to increase the fertility of the soil, and the acreage of arable land, the question of landownerships, the organization of agriculture, etc., all are now critical and interdependent issues. Furthermore the solution depends on the population growth, since the problem is not in producing foodstuffs as such, but in producing food in the amount required by the existing population. Eventually, the availability of food in one part of the world and the desperate need for food in another will create a new international political situation; the very daily existence of the people in the needy parts of the world will depend on the decisions in other parts and over a long period of time, perhaps indefinitely. Then, the basic individual human values and attitudes of the members of the world community will become a determining factor in deciding whether specific tradeoffs and necessary sacrifices will be made. Apparently, the emerging world system requires a "holistic" view to be taken of the future world development: everything seems to depend on everything else. Such a holistic approach is also referred to as the "systems approach," meaning that one looks at the totality of all aspects of a problem rather than focusing attention on an isolated phenomenon, as is the case in the analytic approach traditionally used in scientific inquiry. "You cannot do merely one thing," as G. Hardin has put it. A good example is pollution brought about by anti-pollution devices. The sequence of events started with the explosive growth of industry on the eastern coast of the United States and in Western Europe. Jungles of smokestacks created air-pollution and particle-removing air-cleaning devices were installed to combat that pollution. As a result, smoke pollution was cut down considerably. However, the gases up the smokestacks did not carry solid particles and the various nitrogen oxides and sulfur dioxide could freely combine with water in the atmosphere forming sulfuric and nitric acid. Had the escaping gas contained solid particles the acids would not be formed. So now the rain from the supposedly cleaned atmosphere carried the acids on buildings and crops; a case was reported in which the rain was alleged to have been as acid as pure lemon juice: 1000 times the normal level.

Events surrounding other contemporary crises give equally strong indications of the emergence of a global and increasingly complex world system. The energy crisis quite readily provides another such illustration. When the oil crisis broke out in October 1973 efforts were directed toward resumption of supply flow to meet whatever demands would develop. But that turned out not to be the real problem. The real problem is only appearing now when a continuous increase in consumption coupled with an increased price for oil is bringing a major transfer of wealth and economic power. Iran has already acquired what amounts to a "minority" control of Krupp industries—a major steel-producing and engineering company in Germany. The *annual* excess of revenues to the oil exporting countries will amount to 60 billion dollars, which is about two thirds of all overseas investment which United States firms have acquired up to this date. Using such a one-year surplus they could acquire control of an amazing number of companies in the Western developed world including such U.S. giants as American Telephone and Telegraph, Dow Chemical, General Motors, IBM, ITT, U.S. Steel, and Xerox. And what can be acquired in ten years? The oil exporting coun-

Brief on Emergence of World Resources System†

The developed nations and regions are becoming increasingly dependent on the non-renewable resources from the rest of the world. This can perhaps be best illustrated for the United States which traditionally has been a nation with the most advanced industry and abundance of resources. Until the late 1940's the United States was a net exporter of materials. Starting in the early 1950's the situation changed considerably. By 1970 the deficit due to import of materials reached $4 billion and is projected to climb up to $60 billion annually around the year 2000 (Figure A) assuming no dramatic change in relative prices for materials. Meanwhile the material consumption in the United States as a portion of the total world consumption has declined from 42 percent in 1950 to 27 percent in 1970 (Figure A); so the situation in other developed regions as Western Europe and Japan is getting relatively even worse.

Figure A

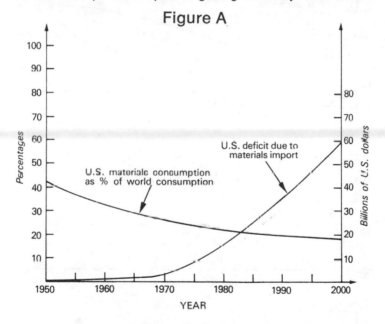

Even more illuminating is the situation regarding some key minerals: In 1970 the United States imported all of its requirements for chromite, columbium, mica, rutile, tantalum, and tin; more than 90 percent of its requirements for aluminum, antimony, cobalt, manganese, and platinum; more than half of its requirements for asbestos, beryl, cadmium, fluorspar, nickel, and zinc; and more than a third of its requirements for iron ore, lead, and mercury.

†*Source:* Material Needs and the Environment Today and Tomorrow: Final Report of the National Commission on Materials Policy, *June 1973, U. S. Government Printing Office, Washington, D. C.*

Figure B shows what percentage of requirements for some basic non-ferrous metals (namely, aluminum, beryllium, copper, lead, magnesium, mercury, platinum, tin, titanium, zinc) and ferrous metals excluding iron, (namely, chromium, cobalt, columbium, manganese, nickel, tungsten, vanadium) has been covered by imports from 1950 to 1970 and the projected increase in import needs through the year 2000. Figures C-F show the past and projected supply and demand relationship for some basic materials. Clearly, without major effort at an unknown cost, which also might be accompanied by the introduction of new economic and production controls and a relative decline in the standard of living, no region can be fully independent.

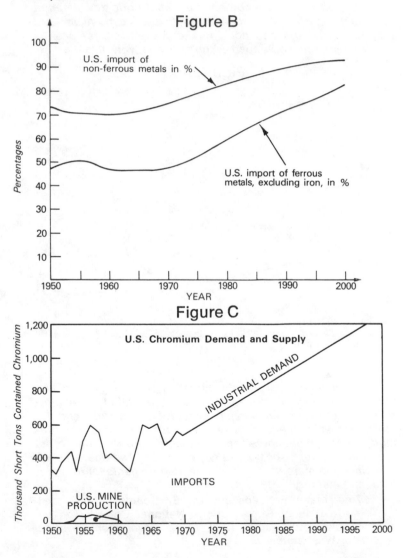

Figure B

U.S. import of non-ferrous metals in %

U.S. import of ferrous metals, excluding iron, in %

Figure C

U.S. Chromium Demand and Supply

INDUSTRIAL DEMAND

IMPORTS

U.S. MINE PRODUCTION

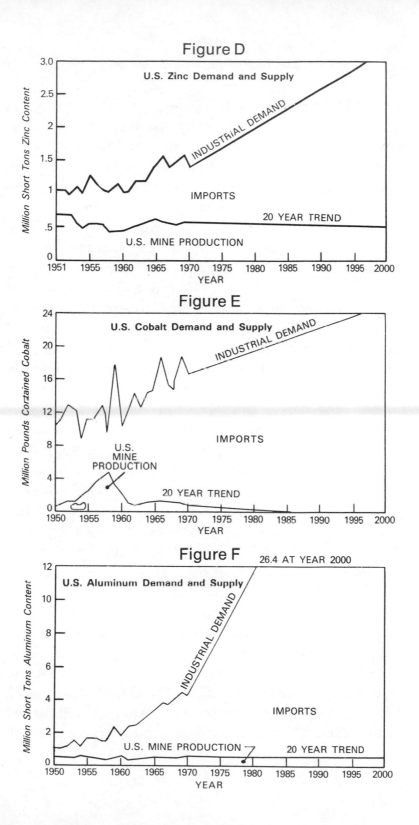

Figure D

U.S. Zinc Demand and Supply

INDUSTRIAL DEMAND

IMPORTS

20 YEAR TREND

U.S. MINE PRODUCTION

Million Short Tons Zinc Content

YEAR

Figure E

U.S. Cobalt Demand and Supply

INDUSTRIAL DEMAND

IMPORTS

U.S. MINE PRODUCTION

20 YEAR TREND

Million Pounds Contained Cobalt

YEAR

Figure F

26.4 AT YEAR 2000

U.S. Aluminum Demand and Supply

INDUSTRIAL DEMAND

IMPORTS

U.S. MINE PRODUCTION

20 YEAR TREND

Million Short Tons Aluminum Content

YEAR

tries will accumulate $500 billion in less than ten years; an amount which can buy twice the total output of the Japanese economy in the mid-sixties and is of the same order of magnitude as the total world monetary reserves. The developed world could consider interfering in the apparent transfer of economic power if it were not in dire need of both oil and capital; increasing size and complexity of industrial plants, specifically in energy-related sectors, make investment programs more difficult for private companies. Only in May 1974 two major U.S. utilities have announced cancellation of previously planned projects for the construction of nuclear power plants. The estimated cost of such a plant has reached $1.5 billion. With the high interest rates imposed to control inflation and an uncertain economy a long-range investment program going into billions of dollars is simply outside the reach of many companies. The alternative to private investment could be government investment programs, which would require increased taxation and would lead to control or nationalization of the energy industry. Another alternative, however, is foreign investment. In such conditions of interdependence neither of the two sides, oil-exporting or oil-importing countries, can plan long-term development without taking into account the development in other regions and indeed the entire globe.

Global interdependence also appears in other areas of material resources. A confrontation between the raw material producers and consumers on a broader front seems to be in the making amid clear signs of ever closer interdependence between the two sides. The United States, which up to the 1940s was a net exporter of materials, will depend by the year 2000 on imports of around 80 percent for all ferrous metals, excluding iron, and 70 percent for all non-ferrous metals. In late 1973 Morocco increased the price of phosphate exports threefold, while in spring 1974 Jamaica increased the taxes on bauxite exports severalfold. The objective was not to inflict economic damage on the bauxite-importing nations but rather to redress the damage done to the balance of payments due to increased oil and food prices.

The reality of the emergence of the world system and its integrative effect on all facets of world development can be also seen by extending the view to the less developed world. The oil import bill of the developing countries will reach $17 billion in 1974, a level more than five times that of 1970. Such an outflow of foreign currency will reduce their total imports by a sizable fraction, cutting into the import of capital goods to build up their industry, and thus hitting where it hurts most: slowing progress toward the goal of reaching the economic takeoff point. Unlike the developed world, the developing countries use imported oil not for the luxuries of individual transportation and home heating, but primarily for agriculture—in mechanization and fertilizer production—and for industry. Whereas the shortage of oil is primarily an inconvenience for the affluent, for underdeveloped countries it means a *direct and immediate* cut in industrial output and food supply. The shortage in oil has already reduced fertilizer production in South Asia in 1973 by hundreds of thousands of tons while over the next three years the tight oil supply situation would certainly lead to an even more dramatic deficit in that region. Regional food production would thereby be curtailed at the time when the demand will have increased considerably. Ten gallons of gasoline, which an average Western citizen uses in one month of pleasure

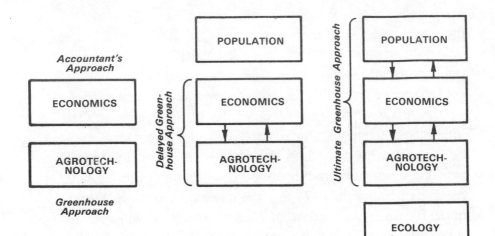

Two approaches to the solution of the world food supply situation are currently in vogue: the first—the accountant's approach—holds that all that is necessary is a 3 percent or 4 percent growth in the economic output. But can the people eat dollars? The second— the greenhouse approach — holds that since it is possible to increase the yield substantially in a laboratory we can feed, for example, 30 billion people. But the question is whether the resources, economic and physical, including infrastructure and other needed support, are available in the regions where such an idealized plan is to be implemented.

Economics and agrotechnology have to be considered simultaneously and in conjunction, i.e., as a system. A realistic assessment can then be made in such a delayed greenhouse approach as to how much food could be produced in what time period in various regions. But the question is how the needs, governed by population development in specific regions, are related to such an increase in food production and nutrition.

Economics, agrotechnology and population development will have to be considered as a system. In such an ultimate greenhouse approach the needed food will eventually be produced. The increase in food production, however, would require that all but a miniscule number of crops — which are needed to support man — be eliminated from the arable land anywhere in the world; and that chemical means be used on an unprecedented scale. But can such a system of drastically reduced diversity in nature, in which a vast majority of species are eliminated, even if achieved at a given time, prevail over a period of time?

Systems Approach

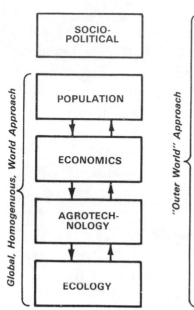

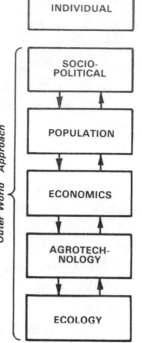

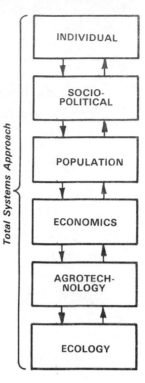

Economics, agrotechnology, population development, and ecology have to be considered as a system. But the world is neither uniform nor monolithic. Eventually the place where additional food can be produced and the place where food is needed will not be the same. Some parts of the world will depend permanently for their very daily existence upon other parts. How will the sociopolitical arrangements be affected by food as a potential weapon?

Economics, agrotechnology, population development, ecology, and global socio-political arrangements will have to be considered as a system. The emergence and continued existence of such a global integrated system would require a change in the attitudes and values which individuals hold with respect to society and world community as well as with respect to the sacrifices needed to protect future generations against major crises.

Economics, agrotechnology, ecology, population, socio-political arrangements, individuals' values and norms have to be considered as a system, in any realistic practical consideration of the world food situation. Anything less than this will not do. It would be highly irresponsible for the generations yet unborn.

driving—is sufficient to produce the food necessary for the survival of one adult. In a situation of worldwide limited supply an increase in oil use decreases food availability. To be sure, the tradeoffs are global, not local. But can one really ignore that when taking a pleasure ride? Energy and food crises, population growth, and economic developments are all becoming tightly intertwined.

In addition to such a tremendously increased complexity of the emerging world system there is yet another characteristic of that system which makes the search for solutions of various global problems increasingly difficult; namely, the necessity of considering much longer time-horizons, looking twenty, thirty, or even fifty years ahead, rather than one, two, and five years as has been customary in the past. This creates a need to act very much in advance of the full development of a crisis, if its potential impact is to be counteracted successfully.

Historically, crisis situations could be looked upon differently. In the first place, the world system was so weakly coupled that local, national, or regional solutions were feasible. Second, once a problem was recognized, there was sufficient time to find a solution, because the rate of change was slow. Even if a full implementation of a solution were to require ten, twenty, or thirty years, the problem was still essentially the same in quality and magnitude as at the time when the solution had been designed. For example, the population in Europe began to grow faster in the early nineteenth century and the specter of eventual starvation was written on the wall by Malthus; but the agricultural yield could be raised by the introduction of fertilizer sufficiently fast so that the problem was solved even before there was a real food crisis. Today, however, the clocks run faster. Knowledge acquired in school or university and experience gained in practice become quickly obsolete. In an exponentially growing situation change develops in much less time than the equivalent changes did in the past. For example, if the annual economic growth is 3.3 percent, the next sixteen years will produce the same change as the past forty years. This might help to explain why political and economic decision-makers have consistently underestimated * future change, for they too have often marched into the future with their eyes on the past. We are indeed living in a very dynamic world in which we have to look decades ahead when making decisions concerning many vital issues. Such a need cannot but require at least some adjustments within a political system based on a four-year election cycle.

All contemporary experience thus points to the reality of an emerging world system in the widest sense which demands that all actions on major issues anywhere in the world be taken in a global context and with full consideration of multidisciplinary aspects. Moreover, due to the extended dynamics of the world system and the magnitude of current and future change, such actions have to be anticipatory so that adequate remedies can become operational before the crises evolve to their full scope and force.

* With an annual 3.3 percent increase the change in the next forty years will be five times greater than the change in the past forty years under the same annual growth conditions.

CHAPTER 4

Multilevel Model of World System

Analysis of the *future* evolution of the world system—any system as a matter of fact—has, in principle, two aspects: objective and subjective. The objective aspects are those based on the relationships describing a system's functioning which are established through experience and scientific analysis as well as the data measured or observed in the past. For example, for an economic system we know that an increase in investment will increase capital stock and, assuming normal economic conditions, will result in an increased economic output; similarly, for a population system it is known that an increase in fertility rates, assuming there is no increase in mortality rates, will result in due time in a faster increase in population level. The subjective aspects are those which refer to the uncertainty that is always present when looking into the future and when dealing with people since their choices on an individual or social level cannot be fully predicted.

The objective aspects of world development are represented in terms of a model, in this particular case a computer model. By a model we simply mean a coherent and systematic set of descriptions of the relevant relationships. The model represents an image of the relevant aspects of reality as we perceive it. Such a model does not have to be given in terms of numbers; it might only indicate what is related to what and possibly in which sequence. Everybody uses models of this kind repeatedly in a variety of situations whenever a decision or choice is to be made. For example, a person is scheduled to fly from Cleveland to Hannover. In the morning he looks out of the window and sees fog completely enveloping the city. His mental image, based on his own experience and what he has heard from others regarding the relationship between fogs, airline schedules, etc., tells him that in such a fog there would be no flights going out. He might decide to go back to bed. On the other hand, if the trip is important he would call the airport to check whether the flight was, indeed, canceled or postponed. This latter decision is also made on the basis of a model which relates the weather conditions at the moment and how they might be at the time of the flight; it also assumes a more precise model developed by technical experts who use actual measurements of various weather parameters and quantitative relationships between them. The difference between the two models lies in the respective degree of precision of each, but they both serve the same purpose, namely, to help decide what future course of events would be most desirable.

We also use a model of the world system in order to

analyze the future evolution of that system. Such a model must, of course, be precise and, because of the enormous complexity and large number * of relationships involved, a computer must be used to determine and calculate all the changes which take place as the system evolves. Hence, we have constructed a computer model which means a set of relationships represented within the computer.

The subjective aspects of world development are dealt with in the way the world system computer model is used to analyze possible future patterns in the evolution of the system. Uncertainty in the analysis of the future is due to the impossibility of predicting *exactly* all conditions under which the system will evolve and all choices which will be made within the system that will influence its evolution. For example, in the illustration considered above, an increase in fertility rates results in a faster increase in population level *assuming* there is no increase in mortality rates, as could happen if an epidemic or mass starvation were to occur. Similarly, an increase in capital stock results in an increase in economic output *assuming* there is a normal supply of labor and normal demand for goods. To assess the future evolution of the system various assumptions must be made regarding possible future events and the computer model then indicates the consequences of such occurrences, i.e., the future evolution of the system under these conditions. *A sequence of possible events and sociopolitical choices is termed a scenario and the method is termed scenario analysis.* Future evolution of the system is analyzed in reference to a set of scenarios. In principle, in such an analysis, we are not trying to predict the future—an effort of rather doubtful value

---

* In our model about 100,000 relationships are stored in the computer, as compared to a few hundred in other well-known world models.

when one is concerned with very long time horizons—but to assess alternative future developments. The likelihood of any future evolution depends on the likelihood of events, which constitute a given scenario taking place in reality. The scenario analysis methodology is apparently more realistic than forecasting or predicting types of methodologies. However, it might appear as "too flexible," i.e., as not leading to define enough conclusions. This is *not* the case! For instance, if the system's behavior has certain characteristics over an entire set of scenarios, i.e., these characteristics appear for every alternative sequence of events, the likelihood of the system having such attributes in the future is considerable. Indeed, if the set of alternative scenarios is broad enough, and if the system has certain attributes persistently in all scenarios, it can be considered as inevitable that these attributes will be observed in the future. For example, assuming that there is no change in fertility and mortality rates, the population in South Asia will increase by one billion people by the end of this century. Assuming, however, a more effective population control program which would bring the fertility rates down to equilibrium level in thirty-five years, the population level would be increased only by some 800 million by the end of the century. Proceeding in the same direction, we conclude by analysis of the model that even the most stringent population control program will still result in an increase of more than a half billion people in that region. It can therefore be considered as certain that in the year 2000 the South Asian population will have increased by more than a half billion people. Furthermore, analysis of a whole set of scenarios from most optimistic to most pessimistic, shows that the increase in regional agricultural production, barring massive foreign aid for agricultural development, would not be commensurate with the population increase. A deficit in food supply in that region can therefore be considered as a certainty.

It is not possible in a general report of this kind to fully describe the model or the methodology of scenario analysis as used in the study.* However, it is helpful to grasp at least the basic structure of the model and the framework in which scenario analysis has been conducted in order to appreciate the results of the analysis as reported in the rest of this book. After all, a key feature which distinguishes our study from many other treatises concerned with the prospects and alternatives for humanity is that our study is not based on ideological considerations, i.e., verbal inferences, but on scientific methodology and actual data. Our approach possesses the following major structural characteristics:

1. The world system is represented in terms of interdependent subsystems, termed regions. This is essential to account for the variety of political, economic, and cultural patterns prevailing within the world system.

2. The regional development systems are represented in terms of a complete set of descriptions of all essential processes which determine their evolutionary, i.e., physical, ecological, technological, economic, social, etc. These descriptions are related through a multilevel hierarchical arrangement reflecting the relevant scientific disciplines.

3. Account is taken of the apparent capability possessed by the world development system to adapt and change

* Such a description can be found in the reports listed in Appendix IV and are available from the International Institute for Applied Systems Analysis (IIASA), Laxenburg, Austria, on request.

Brief on Limits

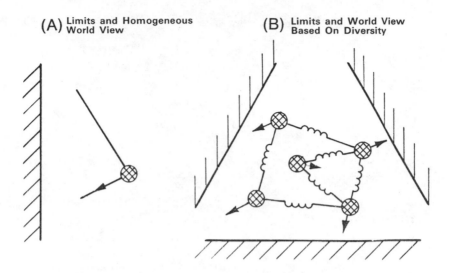

(A) Limits and Homogeneous World View

(B) Limits and World View Based On Diversity

*In the "one-world" or homogeneous view of the world develop-
ment in which differences between various parts in the world
are suppressed and one talks only about global indicators and
variables, the entire system reaches its limits at one time and
either collapses or not. In the world view based on diversity
there is no such concept as one limit for the entire system;
rather, different parts of the system face different limits at different times with the traumatic experiences for the entire
system depending on the interrelationship of the constituent
parts. In a most simplified analogy, the homogeneous world
concept resembles a swinging pendulum, which, in order to
avoid collision with a limit, has to reduce speed and acceleration immediately. In a similar analogy the diversified view of
the world could be represented with a set of balls connected
by a spring system; any of the balls might encounter its own
limits, but others might still be a distance away from their
own constraints. The effect of such a collision will propagate
through the system in relation to the strength of interaction
developed up to that point, that is, depending on the spring
system. At any rate the collapse, if it occurs, would be regional
rather than global, even though the entire global system would
be affected.*

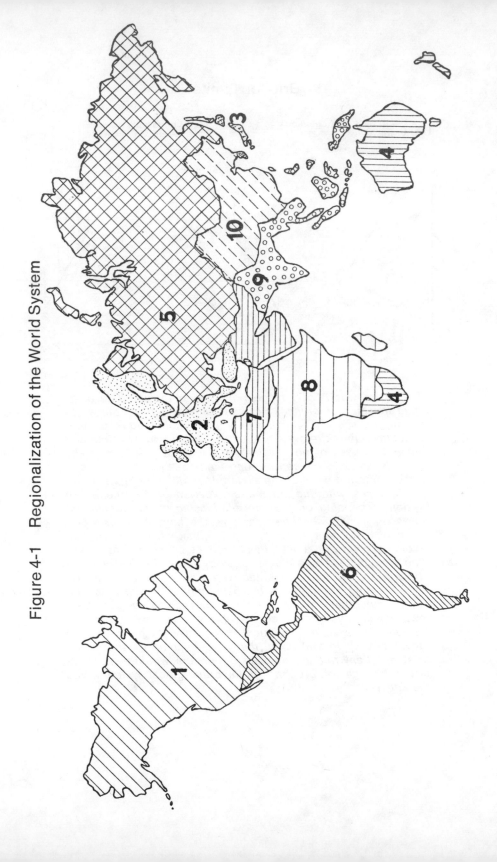

Figure 4-1   Regionalization of the World System

through processes by which calamities which appear to be on the path of future evolution can be averted or minimized.*

The regional view is not antithetical to the concern for comprehensive global development; on the contrary, it is necessary for dealing with the important issues with which the world is and/or will be confronted. Viewing the world system as homogeneous, i.e., describing it in reference to population growth in the entire world, the income per capita as averaged over the entire world, etc., as has been done in earlier world modeling efforts † led to an inaccurate representation of the "mechanism" how the system operates and can be misleading, i.e., lead to the formulation of problems not based on reality and therefore to the prescriptions for solving these problems, which are erroneous (see Brief on Limits). It is essential to acknowledge the fact that the world community consists of parts whose pasts, presents, and futures are different. Hence, the world cannot be viewed as a uniform whole, but must

---

* The difference between viewing a system as a mechanical device or as a living system (or containing living system parts) can be best seen in the implications of taking such different views. As an illustration, let us consider the movement of a car on a highway, some distance from and approaching a barrier. If the car is viewed from "outside" simply as a moving physical object, the recommendation for action would be an immediate reduction in speed. On the other hand, if the "internal construction" of the system is appreciated, that is, if it is acknowledged that the car has a driver, the action recommendation will be to alert the driver. In the first case the action is taken to change the system's overall functioning. In the second case the action is taken to change the system internal strategy. If the system has living parts, as the world system most certainly does, any recommendation for change must take that fact into account.

† For example, see Meadows et al., *The Limits to Growth* (Potomac Associates: Washington, D.C., 1972).

instead be seen as consisting of distinct, though inter-connected, regions. In our study the world system is divided into ten regions as shown in Fig. 4-1: (1) North America; (2) Western Europe; (3) Japan; (4) Australia, South Africa, and the rest of the market economy developed world; (5) Eastern Europe, including the Soviet Union; (6) Latin America; (7) North Africa and the Middle East; (8) Tropical Africa; (9) South and Southeast Asia; and (10) China.* For the sake of simplicity shortened titles will be used on occasion for some regions; in particular Region 4 will be simply referred to as "Rest of Developed," Region 5 as "Eastern Europe," Region 7 as "Middle East" and Region 9 as "South Asia."

The regionalization was made in reference to shared tradition, history and style of life, the stage of economic development, socio-political arrangements, and the commonality of major problems which will eventually be encountered by these nations. The model does not presuppose any formal or informal regional supranational arrangements, although our analysis indicates quite strongly that there exists a need for the establishment of larger communities of nations in the developing world to create a better balance of political and economic power as well as of cultural influence among the world-regions.† Some compro-

* See Appendix II for the listing of the nation-states included in the different regions.

† By way of example, can a balanced formulation of long-term international interests and policies be reached by direct negotiations between such different partners as the United States and Dahomey (2.5 million inhabitants)? In our opinion, certainly not. Just as the European Economic Community was formed to make the European countries a partner with an economic weight equal to the United States, analogous regional communities should also be considered in other parts of the world.

mises had to be made in the process of regionalization and some changes will appear desirable for analysis of specific issues. For example, Region 9 should be subdivided into South Asia, containing Pakistan, India, Bangladesh and Srilanka, and Southeast Asia for detailed consideration of long-term food supply issues. In analyzing some other types of problems, the world system is represented in terms of some clusters of regions obtained from the original ten regions by aggregation. For example, the Developed World (Regions 1, 2, 3, and 4), the Socialist World (Regions 5 and 10), the Less Developed World (Regions 6, 7, 8, and 9). For still other issues only two regions are identified: the "North"—consisting of the Developed World and Eastern Europe, and the "South," consisting of the Less Developed World and China (Regions 6, 7, 8, 9 and 10).

The multidisciplinary set of descriptions of regional developmental processes is structured in a hierarchical arrangement with the levels termed "strata." The stratification in the present version of the world system model is shown in Fig. 4–2. The *environmental stratum* incorporates (a) the geophysical states and processes which are included in what is called man's physical environment: climate, land, water, air, physical resources, etc., and (b) the ecological processes in man's living environment, the plant and animal kingdoms on whose support man's very existence depends and of which man might very well be considered only a part, no matter how prominent. The *technology stratum* embraces all human activities ranging from agriculture to satellite communication—those which in biological, chemical, or physical terms involve mass and energy transfer. *The demo-economic stratum* includes the "accounting systems" humanity has designed to keep track of its numbers and the goods man

Figure 4-2   Computerization of the World System Model

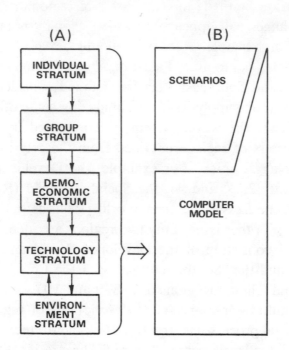

The behavior of the world system is represented on five levels, termed strata (see A): individual, group demo-economic, technology, and environment. Each level provides a representation of the world system using knowledge as embodied in different sets of scientific disciplines, from psychology and nutrition to ecology and geo-physics. All strata are interrelated in a total model.

Not all of the relationships and processes can be represented by a computer model based on the cause-effect kind of linkages. The subjective aspects on the individual and group strata are accounted for by designing a set of appropriate scenarios giving alternative sequences of plausible events and social and individual choices. For example, decisions and choices on the group stratum, regarding population policy would be represented by a corresponding set of scenar- time sequences of gradual changes in fertility rates.

produces and uses—that is, to keep track of demographic and economic processes. *The group stratum* represents the system of institutional responses and societal processes of man as a collectivity. The *individual stratum* reflects man's inner world, his psychological and biological makeup.

We cannot give full justice to a detailed description of the model here. However, an indication of how detailed the model is and how submodels on different strata are connected is shown in the Brief on World System Computer Model.

Our representation of the world system development is obviously man-oriented, since on the final, highest level of the hierarchy we consider the individual's needs and concerns. This does not imply, however, that man can, or even ought, to be the sole arbiter of his destiny. Indeed, his environment on whatever level—economic, ecological, or any other—can very well preempt all the choices he may try to exercise. In other words, no matter what his goals or his actions, the future might be determined solely by the inevitable internal momentum of developmental processes. Also, in certain regions of the world, the social and group norms and goals take precedence over individual strivings. This might be a result of historical developments or be a deliberate choice by the people of the regions. The hierarchy we have used in our model is not designed to promote any particular view or preference as to the existing or developing priorities between individual and social norms in any region. Rather, it is intended solely to account for the variety which prevails in reality.

Finally, accounting for the adaptive behavior of the world system is intimately related with the objective-subjective dichotomy in the assessment of possible future occur-

Brief on World System Computer Model

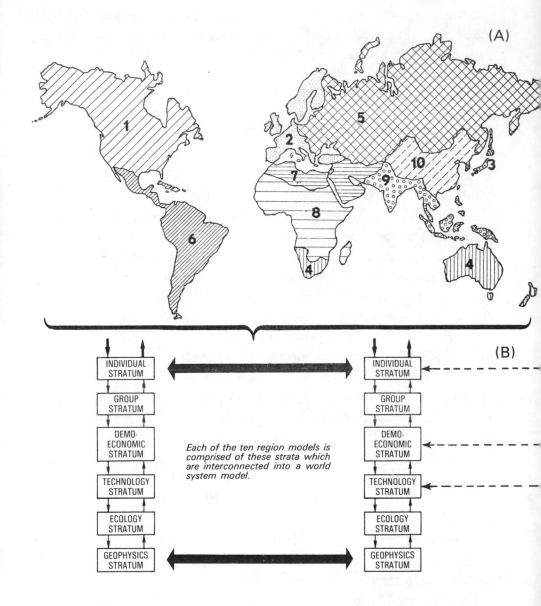

(A)

(B)

Each of the ten region models is comprised of these strata which are interconnected into a world system model.

SIMPLIFIED EXAMPLE OF VERTICAL INTERCONNECTION OF STRATA (D)

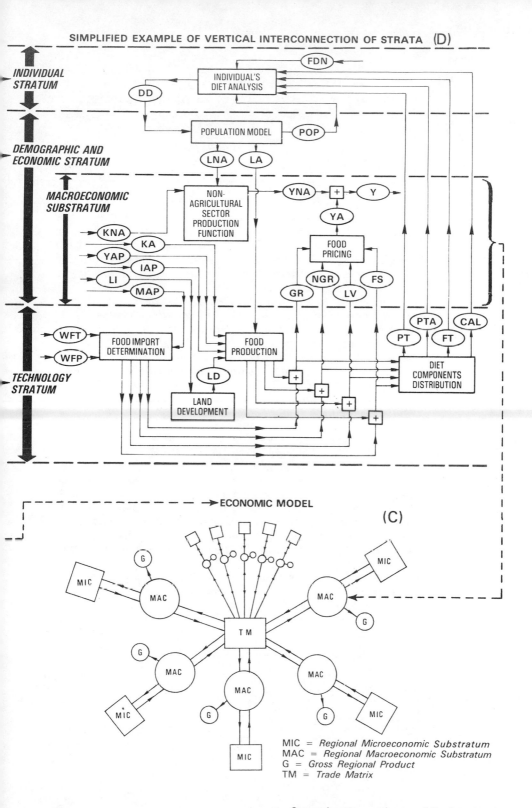

MIC = Regional Microeconomic Substratum
MAC = Regional Macroeconomic Substratum
G = Gross Regional Product
TM = Trade Matrix

See explanatory captions on following pages.

Brief on World System Computer Model

The objective of this rather complicated looking diagram is to give an impression for the technically minded reader as to how the computer model is structured and also to provide a glimpse of its real complexity. The reader not interested in the model per se *can safely skip this brief without losing the continuity of the report.*

The model has 10 regions (Figure A) each represented on six different strata (Figure B). The interdependence of all regional models is expressed through appropriate interconnections and exchange mechanisms. For some strata several representations with different degrees of resolution, i.e., different amounts of detail, are used. For instance, on the economic stratum (Figure C) there is a regional macro economic model given in terms of gross regional product, GRP, and major expenditure components: consumption, investment, government expenditure, etc., and also a micro economic model which specifies the economic output and expenditure components in terms of nine production sectors.

An illustration of how different strata are integrated into an overall world system model is shown in Figure D which presents the interconnections between three submodels — population, economics and agricultural production — for the purpose of food supply analysis. Each of these submodels is quite complicated in itself and only some components and variables of key importance for the interconnections are shown in the figure.

The individuals stratum model determines deficiency in diet for individuals (DD) on the basis of population level (POP), the food diet needs (FDN), and food available given in terms of dietary components; protein (PT), animal protein (PTA), calories (CAL) and fats (FT).

The population model determines the population (POP) in various age groups and labor available for agriculture (LA) and non-agriculture (LNA). The population change is influenced by diet deficiency.

For the sake of simplicity only a portion of the economic model dealing with the production functions is shown in the figure and in terms of only two sectors: agriculture and non-agriculture. The production function for the non-agricultural sector is given in purely economic terms, as the so-called Cobb-Douglas type function, with the non-agricultural labor and capital as the inputs (LNA and KNA) and the level of production of the sector (YNA), as the output respectively.

The production function for the agricultural sector, however, is represented in physical terms on the technological stratum because of interest in the assessment of alternative technologies of food production. It has two basic parts: food production and land development. The main inputs come from the rest of the economic model, namely, investment in land development (LI), investment in agricultural production (IAP), allocation of economic output for technical inputs to agriculture — fertilizer, seeds, etc. — (YAP), available capital (KA) and labor (LA). There are two basic outputs: arable land available (LD), and the food produced expressed in terms of grain (GR), non-grain (NG), livestock (LV) and fish (FS). The level of food import (FM) is determined by the economic output allocated for food import (MAF), food available for world trade (WFT) and world food prices (WFP). The total available food in the region is then analyzed in terms of basic diet components and fed back to the individual stratum model. Finally, the economic value of the regional agricultural output (YA) is obtained from the physical quantities produced and the pricing mechanisms. The sum of outputs of all production sectors gives the total economic output, i.e., the gross regional product (Y).

To appreciate the complexity of the model it should be noted not only that each of the boxes in the diagram, e.g., "population model," is in itself a complicated model but also that an analogous structure is given for all regions and that other submodels, such as energy, are also interrelated in a similar fashion.

rences. The stratified representation as shown in Fig. 4–2(A) is conceptual and cannot be entirely "objectified," i.e., represented by a computer model. This is particularly true for the higher, i.e. group and individual, strata. Only some of the major trends and constraints on these strata could be programmed by means of cause-effect type relationships leaving a good portion to be specified by the scenarios (Fig. 4–2[B]).

Also, we have extended our computer model of the world system still further to reduce the subjective domain of the overall model. This is done in two ways which can be used either in conjunction or separately:

1. The individual and group strata are essentially purposive systems rather than consisting only of cause-effect, mechanistic type processes. We have programmed on the computer some of the decision-processes which constitute the purposive system and the norms which govern the decision, or selection, processes. In this fashion the objective, computerized, part of the overall model has been extended still further by modeling on the computer those options which are available as well as the constraints and conditions under which the decisions must be made.

2. In scenario analysis the future inputs and parameters are specified over the entire time period. In most computer modeling of the future the analyst is but a passive observer during the evolution of the system. This can be remedied by the interactive mode sometimes called "conversational analysis," in which the analyst becomes actively involved during the system's evolution and contributes to a better representation of the adaptive characteristics of the world system. A description of these two important features of our modeling methodology are too technical to be presented here. However, for the interested reader we have briefly described them in Figs. 4–3, 4–4, and 4–5.

In conclusion, several points about our view of the world as reflected in the model and the modeling approach used should be reiterated.

First, the difference between the methodology employed here and prevailing techniques used in other types of computer modeling * should be noted. Our approach is not based solely on a numerical representation of the system nor on an optimization algorithm for narrowly defined criteria. Rather, it includes qualitative and logic-type relationships whenever appropriate, and also relies on the heuristic or interactive approach to decision-making within a framework of institutional, economic, technological, and other constraints. It should be emphasized that the conclusions which one can derive from a study regarding future development of the world system is conditioned in an important way by the methodology used and in particular by the assumed structure of the model (see Brief on Effect of World Model Structure).

Second, the construct we have developed represents in reality a computer-based planning and decision-aiding tool, rather than a computer model in the traditional sense, though to be sure, a model consisting of numerous submodels is part of this instrument. However, it is not a "predictor" but rather serves as an instrument not only to cope with the immense numerical material, but also to extend the user's logic and assess the consequences of implementing his vision of the future.

Finally, some remarks on the behavior of complex systems is in order. It is often stated in reference to the present energy or environmental crises that it looks as though "everything depends on everything else," and, furthermore,

---

* For example: systems dynamics, linear programming, etc.

Figure 4-3   Extended Version of the World System Computer Model

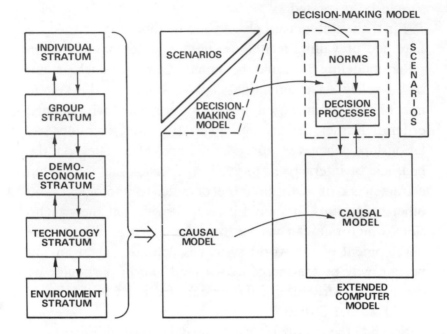

In the extended version of the computer model additional portions of the group and individual strata are represented on the computer. The original version of the computer model is termed "causal model" because it is based on the cause-effect type of relationship. The additional model is termed "decision-making model" because it represents certain aspects of the decision-making activities on the highest two strata which can be computerized. The decision-making portion of the regional system can in turn be represented on two levels: the decision-processes layer and the norms layer. The former reflects the processes of option-selection from among alternatives while the latter represents the constraints and conditions which must be observed in the choice process.

Figure 4-4   Refinement of Decision-Making Model

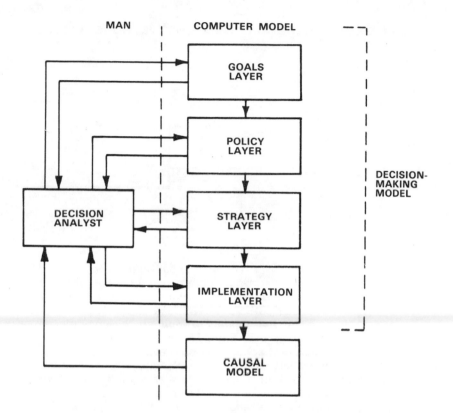

The decision-making model can be refined to represent several
layers of decision-making. In the example shown in the figure
the highest layer contains a set of alternative goals, the layer
below has a set of policies which can be selected to achieve
a selected goal, followed by a set of strategies which can be
used for implementation of a given policy and finally a set of
specific measures which can be used in implementation. The
decision analyst arrives at a set of inputs, necessary for a
computer run, by making appropriate choices, sequentially, on
each of the layers. The number of decision layers depends, in
general, on the type and complexity of the system.

Figure 4-5   Scenario and Interactive Mode Analysis

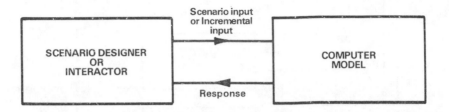

In the scenario analysis a sequence of possible events—termed a scenario — is selected which determines the inputs that are applied to the computer model in order to assess the likely consequences if such events indeed take place. In the interactive or conversational mode the input to the computer is applied incrementally over time. The interactor — a planner, a decision-maker, or a policy analyst — evaluates the effect of previous incremental inputs before selecting the new increment. The analysis is the outcome of a man-machine symbiosis based on a suitable division of labor between them: man decides on priorities, costs, and risks to be taken, while the computer specifies the breadth of options and indicates the likely consequences of decisions.

that this feature of the system is a consequence of its complexity; a complex system thus is considered to be "counter-intuitive," meaning that the system responds differently than what one would expect under usual circumstances; e.g., a measure aimed at improvement would lead in reality to deterioration. From the viewpoint of hierarchically organized or "stratified" systems, however, "counter-intuitive" behavior of a system is not the consequence of its complexity but of *disorder* in the system which, as a corollary, leads to a loss of intuitive understanding of relevant portions of the system which the individuals concerned with that portion of the system have developed through experience and scientific inquiry. Counter-intuitive behavior is therefore a sign that the system is in a crisis and is displaying abnormal behavior. In normal circumstances the strata in a hierarchical system are by and large independent and remain so, as long as the behavior of each of them is satisfactory. In crisis conditions, however, when various strata cannot independently cope with the changes in their environment, they merge together—with the result that every variable on any level becomes dependent on "everything else," i.e., on variables from other levels too and the total system thus becomes counter-intuitive, meaning it behaves differently than in normal conditions from which our intuition is derived. It is only because strata are more loosely coupled in normal conditions that the world appears comprehensible. (How else would progress over so many centuries have been possible?) This observation is important when considering the remedies needed to bring the system out of crisis and into a "normal" condition. What is needed is not to change the path of development by "outside" steering into the direction of further growth or no-growth. What is needed is an *internal restructuring* of the system to restore the "normal" condition where the subsystems are in mutual harmony so that each of them, by solving its own problems, is contributing to the solution of the whole. Such a restructuring leads to the path of organic growth. The analysis of problems and crises as reported in subsequent chapters indicate that: (1) a "horizontal" restructuring of the world system is needed, i.e., a change in relationships among nations and regions and (2) as far as the "vertical" structure of the world system is concerned, drastic changes in the norm stratum—that is, in the value system and the goals of man—are necessary in order to solve energy, food, and other crises, i.e., social changes and changes in individual attitudes are needed if the transition to organic growth is to take place.

BRIEF ON
EFFECT OF WORLD MODEL STRUCTURE ON
PROGNOSIS FOR FUTURE DEVELOPMENTS

*The conclusions drawn from the analysis of the world future development depend on the view of the world as embodied in the structure of the computer model. In an earlier published version of a world system computer model * the world is viewed as a homogeneous system with a fully predetermined evolution in time once the initial conditions are specified. Our view of the world is based on regional diversities, multilevel (stratified) representation of the world system and with evolution in time dependent on socio-political choices as constrained by the prevailing conditions. Each view results in different "prognoses" for the global world future development as embodied in the following theses:*

* J. Forrester, *World Dynamics,* Wright-Allen Press, 1971; Meadows et al., *The Limits to Growth* (Potomac Associates: Washington, D.C., 1972).

Forrester-Meadows Theses

1. *The world can be viewed as* one system.
2. *The system will* collapse *some time in the* middle of the next century *if present trends continue.*
3. *To prevent collapse, an* immediate slowdown of economic growth *must be initiated leading to equilibrium in a relatively short period of time.*

Our Theses

1. The world can be viewed only *in reference to the prevailing differences in culture, tradition, and economic development, i.e.* as a system of interacting regions; *a homogeneous view of such a system is misleading.*
2. *Rather than collapse of the world system as such,* catastrophes *or collapses on a* regional level *could occur, possibly* long before the middle of the next *century, although in different regions, for different reasons, and at different times. Since the world is a system, such catastrophes will be felt profoundly throughout the entire world.*
3. The solution to such catastrophes *of the world system* is possible only in the global context and by appropriate global actions. *If the framework for such joint action is not developed, none of the regions would be able to avoid the consequences. For each region, its turn would come in due time.*
4. *Such a global solution could be implemented only through* a balanced, differentiated growth *which is analogous to organic growth rather than* undifferentiated growth. *It is irrefutable that the second type of growth is* cancerous and would ultimately be fatal.
5. The delays in devising such global strategies *are not only detrimental or costly, but* deadly. *It is in this sense that we truly need* a strategy for survival.

CHAPTER 5

Too Little, Too Late

Having described the world system model used in the analysis of long-range world development, we can now turn to reporting selected results of that analysis. We shall be concerned with the questions posed in Chapter 2 on the strategies for solutions to the crises besetting mankind. How these crises are met will determine whether the emerging world system will be launched on a path of organic growth or will stumble from one crisis to another, and finally into global catastrophe.

In this chapter we shall deal chiefly with the questions relating to the persistency of the crises and to the cost of delays in facing them squarely. We shall consider these questions here in reference to a problem high on the current world agenda: the economic gap between the already industrialized regions (the developed regions), and the regions in the process of industrialization and development (the developing or underdeveloped regions).

Historically, evolution of any human society has been marked by the growth and decline of various gaps between different social groups. If a society is to preserve its integrity, widening of such gaps simply cannot persist; sooner or later the gaps will either be sufficiently narrowed or the fabric of the society will yield to centrifugal forces. Analogously, mankind cannot enter even the first stage of organic global growth if the economic gap between various world regions increases continuously; it is the question of survival of the world as such. The hopes were nurtured at the end of the colonial era that from then on time would be working in favor of narrowing the gap between colonizer and colonized; the vital question is whether these hopes were founded and what, if anything, could be done to speed the narrowing process.

We shall provide answers to these questions by means of a selected set of scenarios depicting alternative paths of future development of the world system. The *first, or standard, scenario* depicts how the gap would change if the historical pattern of development were to prevail. In this scenario the relative level of foreign aid does not substantially increase over the presently prevailing level. To avoid biases that might be introduced by the predominance of population growth factors, we have made a somewhat optimistic though reasonable assumption concerning the success of population policies: namely, it was assumed that the fertility rate in all regions in the world will reach an equilibrium rate * in no more than thirty-five years.

---

* "Equilibrium fertility rate" denotes the rate that, if unchanged, would lead to an equilibrium in the population level after an appropriate

The results of the first scenario computer analysis are rather disquieting. Not only does the economic gap between rich and poor regions not narrow, but it increases considerably in terms of ratios and appallingly in absolute terms. The gap between the average per-capita incomes in the Western industrialized countries grouped according to our classification in the Developed World Region (Regions 1, 2, 3, and 4) and in Latin America (Region 6) will increase from 5 to 1 to almost 8 to 1 or, in absolute terms, from about $2000 to more than $10,000 per capita. The situation in South Asia would be even worse. The per-capita income gap between the Developed World and South Asia (Region 9) and similarly Tropical Africa (Region 8) would increase in absolute terms from nearly $2500 to $13,000 while in relative terms the per capita income ratio will remain above 20 to 1. If one relies on the prevailing economic patterns, trying to close this gap might as well be forgotten (Fig. 5–1). The present trends and attitudes are apparently loaded heavily against narrowing. The crises inherent in the economic gap are clearly not only persistent but even worsening.

Now, to the second question: What can be done to narrow the gap, at what cost, and when? An obvious means would be to provide investment aid to the needy regions. A target proposed by Professor Tinbergen * could be to reduce the gap to 5 to 1 in the more underdeveloped regions, such as

---

transition period, that is, the total number of people will thereafter remain constant at the population equilibrium level, provided also the mortality rate does not change.

* J. Tinbergen, *Two "Clubs of Rome,"* presented at the Symposium "Toward a Global Vision of Human Problems." Tokyo, 1973.

Figure 5-1   Interregional Gap as Projected by Historical Developments

Scenario 1: The diagram shows the tremendously widening economic gap, particularly in absolute terms of income per capita, between the developed regions and Latin America as well as South Asia, as two different representatives of the developing world under the assumption that the present trends continue without change. Due to the very large population increase the ratio of the per capita income in Latin America and in the developed world declines from 1 to 5 to almost 1 to 8 during the next 50 years. In South Asia the per capita income remains at less than 5 percent of that in the developed regions.

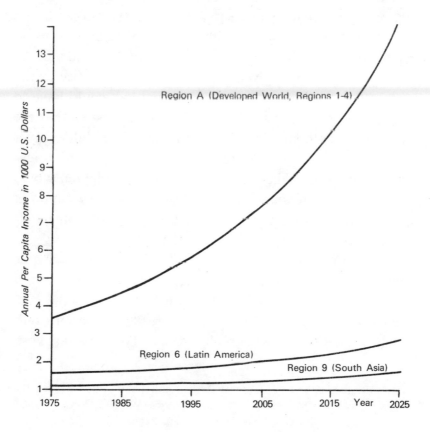

Tropical Africa and South Asia, and to approximately 3 to 1 in the economically more advanced regions, such as Latin America. To achieve that by the year 2000 would be completely out of the question in view of the amount of aid needed, of the corresponding load such a goal would impose on the Developed World, and also in view of the limited aid-absorbing capacity of the developing regions.

In order to assess in more realistic terms the effort needed to narrow the gap, we have designed the *second, continuous aid, scenario* in which it is assumed that continuous aid is provided for the developing regions starting at 1975 over a period of fifty years in order to achieve the Tinbergen target by 2025. The computer analysis of the second scenario shows that the amount of necessary aid * would not be trivial nor could it be given without a certain sacrifice on the part of the developed world. The annual aid would have to reach $500 billion toward the end of the period so that the accumulated amount of aid would reach $7200 billion over the fifty-year period (both figures are in deflated 1963 prices without interest). The load on the developed region would be reflected in an annual loss of almost $3000 per capita in comparison with what could have been achieved otherwise by the year 2025.

Can the political will power of the developed nations be marshaled for such an act? One cannot help but have serious doubts. Perhaps it could be at a later date, when the consequences of the increasing gap become more obvious. What would be the cost of such a delay? To assess that cost,

---

* Given to South Asia, Tropical Africa, and Latin America (i.e., Region 9, 8, and 6 respectively) by North America, Western Europe, Japan, and the "Rest of the Developed World" (i.e., Regions 1, 2, 3, and 4).

Figure 5-2   Closing the Gap Between Developed and Developing Regions Through Investment Aid

Scenario 2: Investment aid is given on a continuous basis for the next 50 years, in order to achieve in Latin America a constant economic growth rate of 7 percent and in South Asia a growth rate of 8.2 percent and thereby reduce by 2025 the per capita income ratio to 3 to 1 and 5 to 1, respectively.

Scenario 4: The same goal is reached at 2025 by massive aid provided only during the 25 years from 1975 to the year 2000, and none thereafter. The investment aid reduces in general the income per capita in the developed world.

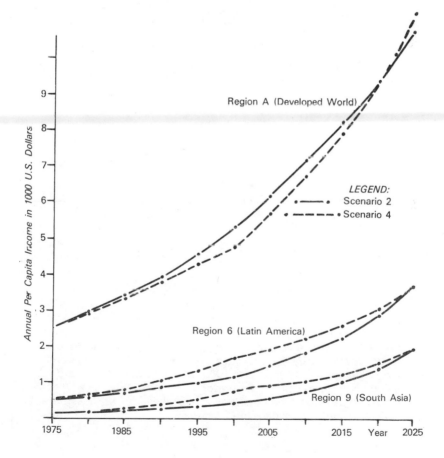

Figure 5-3 Total Annual Investment Aid Provided by the Developed World to Latin America, South Asia and Tropical Africa

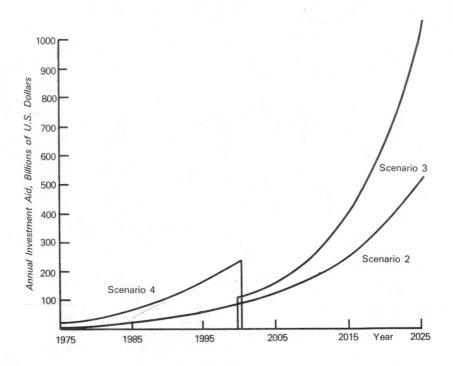

In each of the three scenarios considered here, the aid is given with the purpose of cutting the per capita income ratio between the above — named developing regions and the developed world (Regions 1-4) to 1 to 3 for Latin America and 5 to 1 for South Asia and Tropical Africa. In Scenario 2 aid is given continuously for 50 years, in Scenario 3 the beginning aid is delayed until the year 2000, while in Scenario 4 aid is given only during the last quarter of this century. The enormous advantage of giving aid on a large scale as early as possible (Scenario 4) is only too obvious.

we have designed the *third, or delayed action, scenario* in which it is assumed that the historical pattern of development prevails up to year 2000 and that the attempt is then made to achieve the Tinbergen target by the year 2025. The computer analysis shows that the total necessary aid would be $10,700 billion—more than $3500 billion above the aid level which was necessary in the second scenario. It certainly would be a most expensive delay. It simply does not "pay" to wait.

If delay is costly, would more intensive early action be beneficial, and if so, to what degree? Through such an early action, could the load on the developed world be reduced while achieving the same goal? To investigate that case, we designed the *fourth, or early action, scenario* in which an increased amount of aid is provided in the period from 1975 to 2000 so that no aid is needed thereafter and the Tinbergen target can still be reached by 2025. The results of the computer analysis show that the maximal annual cost reaches "only" $250 billion, while the cumulative cost totals somewhat less than $2500 billion. This means that the total cost of the early action scenario is barely one third of the cost under the continuous aid scenario and little more than one fifth of the cost under the delayed plan scenario. This result is truly stunning: late action costs nearly five times as much as early action. If the investment needs of the developing regions are to be met, the time to act, apparently, is now. However, perhaps the most important aspect of the development aid plan in the fourth scenario is that the developing regions would become fully self-sufficient by the year 2000. The globally beneficial political and economic effect of their early arrival at the economic takeoff point cannot be overestimated.

Figure 5-4 Accumulated Investment Aid (1975 - 2025)

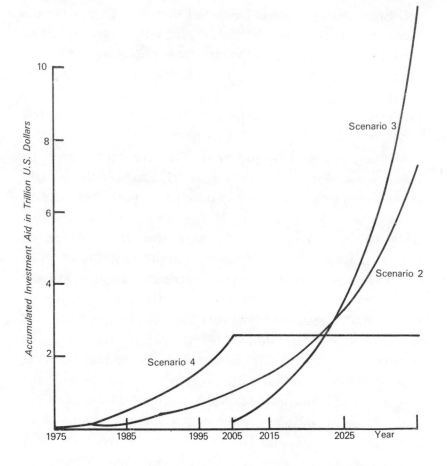

The great superiority of the development aid schedule accord-
ing to Scenario 4 is impressive. It shows how important and,
at the same time, cost saving it is to help the developing coun-
tries as quickly as possible to gain their economic takeoff point.
The cost of aid as measured by the accumulated investment in
the case of early action is less than one fourth the cost in the
case of delayed action.

We cannot leave these considerations without commenting on the "air of unreality" that surrounds this kind of purely economic calculation. First of all, there is the use of the gross regional produce as a measure of economic—and by implication other—achievements of the societies. There is no need here to discuss the inadequacy of a reliance on this criterion as a sole measure of national and regional progress. Alas, no alternative operational measure has yet been designed. Second, in a time of multiple crises, as the period under consideration will most certainly be, one cannot consider any one of the strata in the multilevel world system as fully independent of others.* For example, a change in the raw material demand-and-supply situation will change the technology and pricing structure of industrial and agricultural production so that even if income rises in what might be termed deflated dollars, the real purchasing power, in terms of material goods, will lag significantly behind. The people in the developed world would then not be able to acquire as many additional material goods as the indicated increase in per capita implies. Such restructuring of production cost is already underway as a result of the energy shortage, and it acts as the prime fuel for the current inflation. The inflation spiral might very well persist and even increase in intensity until society is ready to accept the necessary restructuring of production cost, assigning a greater share to the material input, leaving less for labor even at the sacrifice of some individual consumer power.

With such purely economic considerations one only scratches the surface of the real problems in development.

* See also the Brief on Need for Systems Approach in Chapter 3.

Under the surface are the real problems whose solutions are as yet not fully perceived, even assuming that the industrial regions are fully willing to provide the necessary assistance. Actually, present measures of economic development, such as those based on highly capital-intensive industry, might worsen the plight of the poor in underdeveloped regions by increasing the ranks of unemployed and displaced people in large urban areas. What is actually needed is what is called an "intermediate technology," * which requires capital per new job opening approximately equal to the annual income per employee; furthermore, such a technology should not be conditioned by the availability of high quality materials nor should it demand high accuracy, large organizations or long and elaborate training for potential employees. Such a development cannot be realized by a transfer of technology from the developed regions but by the development of a new technology suitable for the process of development as it takes in presently prevailing conditions in the currently developing nations.

Last, but not least, we must question whether such development, as already described in purely economic terms, can take place at all in view of organizational, political, and resources constraints. These questions, again, cannot be analyzed solely within the economic framework; other strata of our world system's hierarchy must certainly be involved.† The change in the availability, location, and cost of various

* E. F. Schumacher, *Small Is Beautiful, A Study of Economics as if People Mattered* (London: Blond and Brigs, Ltd., 1973).

† In this connection see the results of the "squeeze" scenario in Chapter 8 which shows considerable decline in income per capita in case of material, i.e., oil, shortage.

resources will be of such magnitude that even the very notion of developed and underdeveloped economies will have to be revised in at least two ways: First is the question of whether the raw materials and other support for a developed world economy at a 500 percent increase in average per-capita income level will be forthcoming. For example, an economy fully dependent on an increasing flow of certain raw materials that could be cut off on short notice can be considered "overheated" but not properly developed—as "obese" but not as healthy. In traditional economic calculations, material used in production processes is concerned as an output, as e.g., labor, and is treated differently than capital stock, which needs to be "replenished" to keep production going. However, if a material is in a finite supply, it is more appropriate to consider it as a "stock" that is being depleted and, therefore, whose value increases as the remaining stock becomes low. Such an approach would lead to a new approach to economic considerations of production processes. The second question relates to the very notion of "developed" and "underdeveloped" economies which implies that all support is available at any time to bring the undeveloped part to the developed part level. If that were not the case, i.e., if the resources market and other support could sustain the total world economy only at a level below the developed world level, then one has to talk about the overdevelopment of some regions in conjunction with the underdevelopment of others. An example of this dilemma is provided by the oil crisis.

Total energy need in any region is a function of the level and the structure of economic activities. To achieve in the region "South" by the year 2025 even the low level of per-capita income indicated in the scenarios in this chapter, very substantial amounts of energy will be needed because of those regions' population growth rate. It is apparent, then, that the "South" will become a serious competitor for energy resources; for example, the needs of South Asia alone will then be approximately equal to five times those of Western Europe in 1970. But where are these resources to be found at that time and at what cost? Will the most convenient energy source, oil, even be available? The indications are that it won't. Our model shows that if oil demand follows the historical pattern of development, even with optimistic estimates of the reserves, natural oil will be completely used up sometime early in the next century.* New sources of energy will surely be developed by then. But the indications are, in the absence of a major scientific and technological breakthrough, that the substitutes will not only be more costly but also much less adaptable to the needs of the yet undeveloped nations. Meanwhile, the developed nations will use the natural oil during the remaining decades at an excessive rate and fully out of proportion to to the rest of the world, buying time for the development of substitutes without undue economic penalty. If every nation were to use oil at the same per-capita rate as the developed world, our computer simulation indicates that the entire world reserves would be used up by 1982; if oil discoveries continued at the same rate as in the preceding decades, the reserves would be exhausted by 1985, much too early to have energy substitutes ready to take the place of oil.

The industrialized world is thus granted the time to de-

---

* See Appendix III(B), "Brief on Fossil Fuel Reserves."

velop alternative energy sources only by using nearly the entire world oil reserves and by that action preempting the supply of the most efficient and convenient energy source precisely when the developing nations need it most.

Should that not be taken into account in the current reassessment of allocation of oil consumption and of materials consumption in general? Isn't it legitimate to ask, as representatives of the developing countries, whether there should be maximum limits on consumption of materials which have finite reserves, such as oil? A more equitable long-term allocation of global world resources would require that the industrialized regions put a stop to further overdevelopment by accepting limits on per-capita use of finite resources. If development aid is to lend a truly helping hand to the hungry billions who must find a way out of their poverty, more than investment capital is needed. Unless this lesson is learned in time, there will be a thousand desperadoes terrorizing those who are now "rich," and eventually nuclear blackmail and terror will paralyze further orderly development. Now is the time to draw up a master plan for organic sustainable growth and world development based on global allocation of all finite resources and a new global economic system. Ten or twenty years from today it will probably be too late, and then even a hundred Kissingers, constantly crisscrossing the globe on peace missions, could not prevent the world from falling into the abyss of a nuclear holocaust.

CHAPTER 6

Deadly Delays

"They die so gracefully . . ."

The analysis of the economic gap in the preceding chapter showed the persistence of the present crises and the cost of postponing the actions necessary for their solution. Yet this is not the only worry, nor is the economic cost the only cost incurred. Whether or not to embark on the path of organic growth is a question of mankind's very survival and delays in acknowledging this are life-and-death issues. Nowhere else can this be seen so clearly as in the dilemma involved in population growth.

The greatest danger in the path of a population crisis solution is the tendency to delay the necessary action. "A problem postponed is a problem half solved," Churchill is quoted as saying at the height of the Battle of Britain. He was confronted with apparently imminent defeat, and as long as defeat could be postponed, there remained a chance of winning or at least surviving. However, not all disastrous situations are so clear-cut. Too often the conditions are more subtle, and while postponement of a solution to the problem indeed delays the effort of facing up to the unpleasant choices, time so gained only compounds the problem which becomes increasingly difficult to solve. Such an approach is taken with some logic by too many officials elected or appointed for a limited time. If one invests time and resources in a crisis solution that will bear fruit only after one's term of office is over, the likelihood is that one will get no credit and all the blame; the credit will go to the successor during whose term the benefits accrue, while the blame will be put on the early period during which, in spite of all the resources committed, the solution did not materialize. The fine thread connecting early action and much later fruit is too often lost. The tendency therefore prevails to postpone consideration of the problem until one's term in office has ended and it becomes somebody else's worry. In personal life, however, we know better. We learn, sooner or later, that the choices we face are invariably limited and *diminish* with time. The opportunity one misses at a given time can be regained only at substantial cost at a later date, if at all. In the life of nations, on the other hand, we assume that something, somehow, sometime later, will turn out to save the day. Indeed, it is felt too often that the future will certainly bring increased choices and new opportunities. That is undoubtedly a legacy of an era in which the steady march of progress was taken as an article of faith. In subscribing to such a religion one tends to overlook that there is absolutely no evidence that similar progress will occur "automatically"—by necessity. While the optimism is based on past successes, the past must be taken only as a guide for the future. The past is not the future, and what has happened in the past is not to be assumed to be likely in the future. As Heraclitus stated: "It is not possible to step into the same river twice"; the river flows and the water is constantly changing.

We will consider two questions in the context of the population crisis: Are the choices increasing with time and should we therefore postpone the search for a solution? Granted that we have to be mindful of the things to come, should we not wait until the signs are unmistakable and only then act? Unfortunately, the answer to both questions is no! The reason for the negative answer to the first question is the magnitude of the ensuing crises and the rate at which they multiply; the reason for the negative answer to the second question is the presence of delays in the world system that require actions of "anticipatory" rather than "feedback" nature. That is, actions must be taken even before the contours of the outcome are fully visible, else it becomes too late. We shall prove the validity of these answers by the scenario analysis of the population crisis using our world system computer model.

The incredible acceleration of growth in total world population is perhaps best illustrated by pointing out that if the present rate prevails, more people will be added during *one* year in the middle of next century than during the fifteen hundred years after Christ's birth (Fig. 6–1); and that will be an annual addition becoming even larger as time progresses.

However, the development of the total world population is still a somewhat abstract concept. For too many of us it just means that somewhere else and sometime in the future there will be many more people. The issue is, in fact, much more immediate, for the present pace of population growth

Figure 6-1　World Population Growth

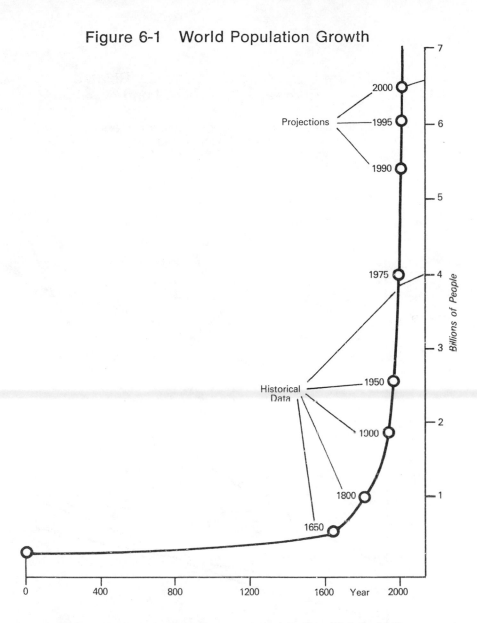

It took more than the first sixteen centuries after Christ's birth for the world's population to increase from 200-300 million to the half billion mark, that is, to double in size. In the next two hundred years another half billion was added and yet another full billion in a mere hundred years, with the population reaching 2 billion at about 1930. In less than a half century, 45 years to be more accurate, the population will have increased by another 2 billion. To add 2 billion more it will only take another twenty years, with the world population overshooting the 6 billion mark in the year 2000.

Figure 6-2   Population Density Related to Area of Cultivated Land

The graphs demonstrate clearly the increased pressure on the food production system which various developing regions will face unless they initiate an effective population policy that would lead to equilibrium fertility by the end of the century.

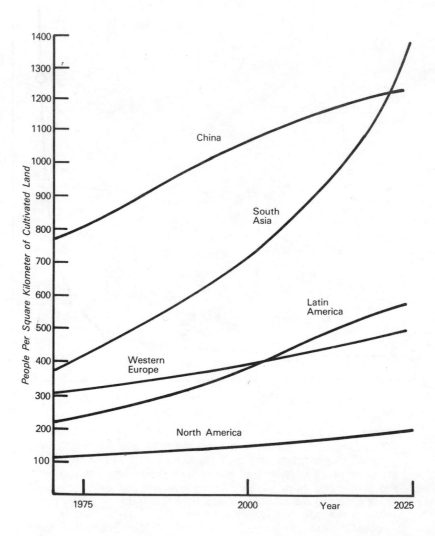

means that the world population would double even within the lifetime of those who are presently in their middle years. In order to gain a better understanding of the meaning of such a population growth and the pressure it creates on the economic, social, and ecological supporting system, one has to look where these additional people will be located, that is, at the change in population density. To assess these changes by using today's population growth rates would yield hair-raising numbers that, it is to be hoped, are too pessimistic. More realistically, therefore, we have assumed that some population policy is being implemented. Specifically, we have assumed that in all world regions the fertility rate declines to an equilibrium level within a fifty-year period, which means that if the fertility rate does not change thereafter the population level will reach equilibrium after an appropriate delay. To focus on the population issue as such, we have also assumed that all support necessary for the increasing population will be forthcoming, that is, there will be no large-scale food shortages to cause massive starvation. The computer analysis indicates that under such conditions at the end of the present century there will be, compared to the year 1970, an additional four people per square kilometer in North America, but 140 people will be added to the same area in South Asia (Region 9). This *increase* alone is more than 60 percent higher than the *present* population per square kilometer in "overpopulated" Western Europe, where there are at present eighty-five people per square kilometer. How that will strain regional resources is indicated by the fact that in the year 2000, for each square kilometer of *cultivated* land in South Asia there will be 390 *additional* people to feed—compared with an additional thirty-seven people per square kilometer

Figure 6-3   Growth of Urban Population
(> 20,000 inhabitants)

The growth of urban population will increase in the developing countries especially after the turn of the century when the rural areas will no longer be able to absorb local population increases. This will have the most serious repercussions in the urban labor market, where in the next 50 years nearly one billion new jobs will have to be created in order to absorb the increase in urban population. If the industrial growth rate should be only 4 percent per year, for example, in South Asia (Region 9) alone the number of unemployed urban people would rise to 100 million in the year 2000, and to more than a half billion in 2025, should the present population growth rates persist.

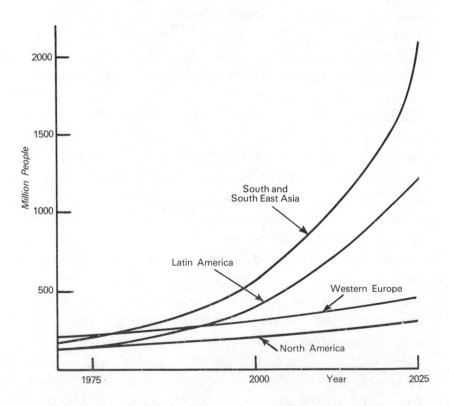

of cultivated land in North America. To top all this, the rate of growth of urban population in South Asia is twice the growth rate of the total regional population. According to Tarzie Vittachi, the Executive Secretary of World Population Year for the United Nations, ". . . if Calcutta grows at its present rate—there would be *sixty million* people just struggling for survival on the banks of the Hooghly at the end of this century."

What is to be done? Is this a Churchillian-type situation in which delay is pregnant with the solution or, at least, it can open an easier or less painful way of solving the problem? Unfortunately, quite the opposite is true. *The longer we postpone the necessary adjustments, the more costly the penalty will be in human suffering and lives.*

To illustrate this crucial point we have designed several scenarios with alternative population policies which enabled us to assess the consequences of various delays as they might occur. A quite detailed population model is used in which the distribution of population by one-year age increment is taken into account for each of the regions and fertility and mortality is represented also in references to the region-specific age distribution.* Such a model enables us to assess the effectiveness of various population policies in a quite realistic manner. The results of our analysis we shall present here in reference to the two most aggregated regions: the "North," which comprises the industrialized part of the world (North America, Western Europe, Eastern Europe including the Soviet Union, Japan, Australia, Oceania, and South Africa), and the "South," which comprises the rest of the world.

* See also Appendix III(D), "Age Structure and Population Growth."

According to the *first, standard scenario* projected on the basis of the historical pattern of development, by the end of this century there would be more people in the "South" region than in the entire world today; in another twenty-five years there would be more than three times as many as in the world today. The population figures thereafter, if the historical pattern continues, are so astronomical as to be almost ridiculous to consider. There is no question whether such development will take place or not. Most certainly it will not! The only questions are whether the slowdown of population growth would be the result of a deliberate population policy or the result of Malthusian checks and what would be the relative cost of the two outcomes.

To investigate a more realistic situation, we have designed the second scenario in which a fully effective population policy is applied starting in 1975 and aimed at bringing the fertility rate over the entire region "South" to an equilibrium level in thirty-five years and to maintain it at that level. Two important conclusions resulted from the analysis of this scenario: first, the equilibrium in "South" is reached only seventy-five years after the initiation of the population policy and forty years after the goal of equilibrium fertility has been reached; second, the equilibrium level is more than twice as high as the level when the policy is initiated. *The need to look at least fifty years ahead when considering the development of the world system is amply demonstrated.*

How about the urgency of action? What would be the consequence of delaying the action until a more opportune time, and what would be the cost of such a delay? To investigate this, we have designed a third scenario, in which the same population policy is applied as in the second, but

Figure 6-4 Population Equilibrium for the Developing World

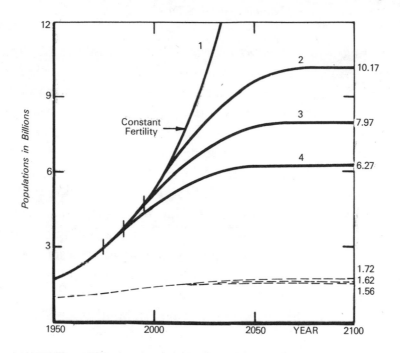

Population in the developing regions has undergone an accelerated growth in the sixties. Were this growth to continue
(Curve 1) at the present pace, only 50 years from now the
population of the Third World would amount to 10 billion people and even an effective equilibrium policy would not then
stop population growth before the 20 billion mark was reached;
of course, provided these masses of people could be fed and
cared for so that starvation, malnutrition and disease would
not stop such growth long before. The effect of an equilibrium
policy beginning in 1975, 1985 and 1995 was investigated and
the results are depicted by the solid curves 2, 3 and 4, respectively. Due to the age structure of the population in the developing countries (see Appendix III on "Age Structure and
Population Growth") population equilibrium is then achieved
at a level more than 100 percent higher than the population
size at the initiation of such policy. Were a policy with a 35
year transition period to equilibrum fertility initiated now, in
the population in the developing world would increase eventually to 6.3 billion, an increase of about 110 percent over
today's population. (This is to be compared with only a 30 percent increase in the developed world with the same equilibrium
policy, see broken curves.) A delay of 20 years in the beginning of such a population policy would lead to an equilibrium
population of 10.2 billion people, i.e., nearly 4 billions larger;
at approximately 3.5 times the present population. Depending
on the beginning date of the equilibrium policy, the ratio of
population in the developing world to that of the industrialized
countries (see broken curves) will change from the present 2.5
to 1 to 4 to 1, 5 to 1, or 6 to 1, respectively.

starting with a ten-year delay, that is, 1985 rather than 1975; finally, a fourth scenario was designed in which the same population policy starts at 1995. The analyses of the computer runs show that a ten-year delay will increase the equilibrium population in the region "South" by 1.7 billion, up to 8 billion people, while yet another ten years will push the population in the "South" over 10 billion. This all is to be contrasted with the slightly more than 2 billion population level in that area in 1950. But the cost that will have to be paid for the luxury of postponing the beginning of action cannot be adequately grasped by looking at abstract population numbers. We are talking about humans, and the cost must be assessed with reference to specific locations and in human rather than economic terms. In South Asia alone the present increase of the potential labor force amounts *every week* to more than 350,000 people, a number that would have risen by the end of the century to 750,000 per week or 40 million people in a year. That is a number twice as large as the total present population of Canada. Ten year later the potential labor force of South Asia would increase by 1 million people per week. The pressure which such a development would put on the socio-political and economic systems is only too obvious, especially if the trend toward urbanization continues to swell the urban areas with a population not only without work but possibly without any hope of improving their lot. To quote T. Vittachi again, "To cope with the population increase, India needs to build 1000 new schoolrooms every day from now on for the next twenty years, 1000 new hospital wards every day from now on for the next twenty years and 10,000 houses every day from now on for the next twenty years."

But this trend could not continue unchecked either. Individual sufferings, most likely coupled with socio-political breakdowns, will be the preventive force. An "indicator" of such sufferings would be the number of additional deaths of children attributed to malnutrition and starvation and which will result from a delay in implementation of an effective population policy. To examine this we have designed a fifth, sixth, and seventh scenario in which South Asia, by the logic of world political development or because of the deliberate political decision of her leaders, relies almost completely on her own resources to support the growing population. In the fifth scenario it is assumed that an effective population policy starts at 1990, while in the sixth scenario the same policy is initiated with an additional five-year delay, i.e., in 1995. The impact of such a delay on the total number of child deaths is quite significant. In cumulative terms, about 170 million additional children would die until the year 2025, if the same population control policies went into effect only five years later. On the other hand, advancing the starting time to 1975, the sum of child deaths would be decreased by more than 500 million.

Perhaps the most shocking aspect of such analysis is that these "overall statistics" hardly portray the truly tragic state of affairs. By letting the "natural feedback" mechanisms of malnutrition and starvation check population growth, the same result, that is, the same overall level of population, could be achieved as through a successful population policy. But what a tragic difference for individual families as well as for the collective quality of the survivors' lives.

The answer to the second question posed at the beginning of this chapter is therefore only too apparent. The delays in coming to grips with the *world problématique* are truly deadly. In Calcutta there is a hospital where special care is provided for children who are found dying of starvation. All efforts are made to ease their last days. "They die so gracefully," the head nun has been quoted as observing. But they die nevertheless. The death of an individual is a tragedy, while the death of a million is statistics—so cynics have been saying. But the death of hundreds of millions could very well mean unprecedented tragedy for the entire world. *The increasingly strong interactions in the world system will provide for precisely that kind of outcome.*

CHAPTER 7

Tug of War for Scarce Resources

By now we have established the persistency of the world crises and the urgency of action if the cost of bringing about desired solutions is to be kept at a reasonable level in economic and in human terms. There remains the question of the nature of the relationships between various parts in the emerging world system. Will the system be characterized by dominance or genuine partnership? The constraints imposed by the various crises cannot but create conflicts. Must these conflicts be resolved by confrontation, or is cooperation possible?

These questions will be considered in the present and following chapters. It should be realized that the conflicts considered here result from competition for resources—materials, energy, food, land, water, air, etc.—in the broadest possible sense. If the resources were unlimited, there would be a chance to avoid conflict. The very phenomenon of growth on our finite planet, however, implies competition for resources; therefore growth can only create circumstances conducive to conflict.

Until the very recent past the fate of people and nations was determined in large measure by the availability of resources necessary for the survival or preservation of the prevailing style of life. Nomads moved constantly in pursuit of food, the most precious of all resources. Advancement in transportation allowed certain societies to extend their hold, by trade or conquest, and to bring the necessary materials home rather than having to move in endless pursuit of them. Frontiers were constantly opened to extend their hold on these necessities. Yet, this period has ended and now the rules of the game have undergone change again. Today, throughout the world, the sites of essential resources and the locations where these resources are most needed are within the boundaries of societies with different, even conflicting goals and objectives. For example, Japan imports 99 percent of its oil, primarily, from the Middle East, to satisfy 65 percent of its total energy needs. In a slightly less dramatic position, Western Europe is still very much dependent on the Middle East, and this dependence will increase substantially and rapidly in the years to come. Even with its great size and the diversity of its geography, the United States is requiring more and more resources from without. Twenty years ago the United States was virtually self-sufficient in the essential raw materials needed for industrial production. According to the National Materials Policy Commission, the United States will, by the year 2000, depend on imports for more than 80 percent of these materials. At the same time, some regions of the world—South Asia and Tropical Africa in particular—will depend to a critical degree on North America and Australia to produce their food.

For a short time in history it seemed—at least in some parts of the world—as if man had finally mastered the fundamental problem of resources development, and was entering a long era of abundance. But now the world is again approaching an era of scarcity. Two types of conflicts are emerging: the first between the short-range and the long-range view of the situation, the second between users and suppliers.

There is always a tendency, fueled by immediate needs, to seek short-term gains even at the expense of long-range benefits. Grave consequences can result, also, if a satisfactory short-range situation is mistaken for a long-range one. For example, the abundance of food, which was heralded several years ago, has proven to be very short-lived. The assumption of this abundance allowed the population to increase, skyrocketing the food need and bringing back the prospect of scarcity. Similarly, the abundance and availability of cheap energy sources, particularly of oil in the 1960s, was taken as a permanent and irreversible state. That misperception inevitably led to the present energy crisis.

Regarding the users' and suppliers' conflicts, two kinds of participants have emerged: those who have resources and almost nothing else, and those who have everything except resources. In the past the dice were heavily loaded in favor of those with knowledge and power—brains and swords: what they could not invent they took. But that is changing. National and regional needs have increased in kind and quantity to the extent that neither inventions nor conquest by force or trade can satisfy these needs. A primary reason for this development was reliance on a pattern of economic

thinking which heavily discounted future costs * and therefore did not prepare for future scarcities. Thus, the developed
world used cheap oil to spur its economic growth, resulting
in a greater demand for oil, which in turn, by remaining
cheap, pushed growth to still higher levels. The spiral continued without regard for safety. The developed world now
seems to be "hooked" on oil; to kick the habit can only be
painful. No substitutes were seriously developed since oil
was deceptively cheap. Allocations and use of oil were governed solely by the immediate cost of getting the oil out of
the ground. No notice was taken that the quantity of oil was
finite and that we were burning, in a split second, often for
frivolous reasons, resources which took nature millions of
years to produce. This situation provides a perfect illustration of arrogance in the contemporary man-nature relationship.† Now that the positions of supplier and user regions

---

* Assume an interest rate of 7 percent. Then, the expenses for anticipatory measures to be taken in order to avert a crisis, that is expected to
occur in the "distant" future, could apparently be reduced to only twenty-
five percent of the present outlay, if one would wait 20 years with their
implementation.

† More examples of the discounting of long-term costs and of the same
disregard for natural processes can be found in the use of many other
essential commodities. Take, for example, medicine as an essential commodity. The present state of medical art has been attained through a
long and extremely costly evolution of medical knowledge and scientific
discoveries, full of success and failures. And what has been squeezed
out of nature, often with painful effort, is now used to interfere with
natural processes, frequently without regard for the total and long-term
effects. Medical advancements obtained through a long process have
been used to reduce mortality almost overnight, historically speaking,
without considering the fertility side of the equation; that opened the
gap between fertility and mortality which is leading to a soaring population—an explosion which, if unchecked, can truly lead to collapse,

have been reversed, the industrial world will have to pay for their former attitude, and not only in the form of high oil prices.

The resolution of conflicts of resource allocation depends on the mechanism used for conflict resolution, which in turn depends on the seriousness of the situation, and the degree of dislocation in the "normal operation of the system." In this chapter we shall consider the least upsetting type of crisis: one whose resolution could be based solely on economic considerations. Implicitly, this presupposes that substitutes for scarce or depleted resources can always be found in time to prevent major technological and economic dislocations. The solution of the resources allocation problem can then be obtained by means of the pricing mechanism. In the subsequent chapters, which deal with more intense conflict, the need for a more comprehensive attack on such situations will become apparent. Indeed, nothing short of a complete integration of all strata, from individual values to ecology and mineral resources—and on a global scale—will suffice for the solution of the world food crises considered in Chapter 9. If mankind is to proceed on the path of organic growth, and if we are to avoid excruciating pains in the transition process—in the form of regional catastrophes for

---

ultimately defeating the whole purpose for medical intervention in the first place: the saving of lives. What good is it to save a human from disease only to watch him die of starvation? Cynics have calculated that for every child saved from starvation today there will be three who will die from the same cause later in this century. Of course such calculations are revolting and fully unacceptable! But the facts behind them should not be ignored either. Help is meaningful only if it is given fully and completely; an intervention in the natural processes should be made only after the full range of side effects has been assessed.

example—conflicts on all levels of intensity ought to be resolved through cooperation, rather than confrontation.

We shall present here the case of oil as a *cause célèbre* of
non-renewable resources. For a considerable period the
worldwide allocation of oil was essentially regulated by a
buyers' market. Now the pendulum has swung, and the
market strongly favors sellers. During the buyers' market
era, high pressure was exerted by the entire world economic
system to keep the price of oil down. Should the situation
become completely reversed in the newly created sellers'
market conditions? Should the oil-exporting regions raise
the price of oil to the limit? In the long run, would a further
price increase over the present level really hurt anyone, and
conversely, would an endless increase in price benefit anyone? How strong a "squeeze"—for example, by withholding
production—should the resource-rich regions apply in pur-
suing their own best interest? It is the emphasis on the "long
run" that is crucial when considering these questions; while
the "short run" situation is often fairly clear, the real dilemma is whether the pursuit of short-term gains leads to the
sates for long-term losses or to the long-term gains. Although these questions have been posed with reference to
the "oil crisis," the same dilemma exists in connection with
any other scarce resource; the lesson learned from the oil
crisis will thus have an implication for food and other
scarce resources.

To analyze the prospects for dealing with the oil crisis, we
have used our world system computer model. In any given
year, the energy needs for each of the regions are determined by the desired economic growth and intended industrial development. The regional oil needs are then computed
as a fraction of the total energy requirements according to

the historical pattern of oil use and postulated technological changes. The difference between production capacity and needs determines whether the given region is a net exporter or importer of oil. The allocation of the available world supply is achieved through a world oil market model. Each scenario is determined by one of the options that the region may exercise in pursuit of its own goals.

The goals of the oil-exporting regions are assumed to be:

1. Achievement of maximum economic growth. This depends not only on the region's ability to produce oil, but to absorb investment.

2. Maximization of the amount of excess revenues that can be used to accumulate wealth outside the region.

3. Increase in the lifespan of the total oil reserves.

The range of alternative actions available to the exporting regions includes:

1. Increase in oil prices during sellers' market conditions. Both the maximum price achieved during the period of consideration and the rate of increase must be evaluated.

2. The withholding of oil supplies by limiting production to a level below the demand. This could be done in a number of different ways—by imposing a ceiling of, say, 10 or 15 billions of barrels per year; by reducing the production to satisfy only a certain percentage of the total demand; by the combination of these and other measures.

3. The use of excess revenues—those which remain after essential imports are paid for—as an economic and political instrument. These funds could be used for investment in other regions, including the oil-importing regions, or could in fact be deliberately withheld from the importing regions.

In the oil-importing regions, as far as the oil crisis is

concerned, the goal is to ensure continued economic growth without interruptions caused by oil import fluctuations, due to actions, such as listed above.

The range of options available to the importing regions include:

1. Increase in regional oil production.

2. Development of alternative sources of energy as substitutions for oil.

3. Reduction of energy demand through conservation measures.

4. Increase in the cost of goods—in particular the capital investment goods—needed by the oil exporting countries. Such an increase can result from competitive pressures for those goods on the world market; or it can be a deliberate act of retaliation for the oil price increase. This latter option could, among others, take the form of export taxes applied selectively to goods imported by the oil-producing regions.

Based on the comparative goals and options available to the producers and users of oil enumerated above, a very severe conflict could quite easily appear and lead to serious dislocations in the world economy. In the realities of the world political situation, conflict can be avoided only if preventative measures do not require lopsided sacrifice on the part of either the oil-exporters or -importers; solutions must be mutually beneficial. Since our concern was with long-range rather than temporary advantages, we used a fifty-year time period to evaluate the possible gains to the exporting regions, namely:

1. The level of their economic attainment, as reflected in the gross regional product, GRP, in the year 2025.

2. The total wealth accumulated abroad by the exporting

regions over the entire fifty-year period, or between 1975 and 2025.*

We shall present the results of the computer analysis relevant to the Middle East, i.e., the Region 7. The gross regional product which the Middle East can achieve by 2025 is a function of the maximum oil price attainable during the next fifty years. To investigate the behavior of this function, we designed a set of scenarios in which the price of oil is increased yearly until it reaches a level specific for any given scenario and then remains constant for the rest of the period. For each scenario there is therefore a characteristic maximal oil price that is assumed to be reached during that period. The results from the entire set of such scenarios can be summarized as follows (Fig. 7–1):

If the price of oil remains at the initial level, the gross regional product of Region 7 reaches about 1.2 trillion U.S. dollars in 2025. As the scenario specific maximal oil price increases the region 7 GRP in 2025 increases too—but only up to a point. In the scenario with the maximal oil price around 50 percent greater than the initial value, the GRP in 2025 becomes $2.7 trillion—or more than double of what was in the scenario with no price increase. However, in the scenario with still higher increase in oil price, the output of our world systems model indicates a decrease in 2025 GRP in the Region 7. This decrease reflects the fact that too great a price rise would make oil prohibitively expensive; consumer-nations would have to find substitutions or do without. If, for example, the maximal oil price

* Economic output is measured here in terms of prices deflated to the 1963 level so as to eliminate the effects of inflation and account only for real economic changes.

Figure 7-1 Economic Growth and Accumulated Wealth of Middle East (Region 7) as Function of Oil Price

An increase of price for a raw material under sellers' market conditions seems to offer nothing but gains for the party in a monopolistic position. However, a deeper analysis of the world system shows that this situation exists only for a very short period. A number of counteracting forces — due to limitation of resources, substitution, development of alernative sources, change in technology, the change in economic conditions, etc — prevent more than a reasonable gain in the long run and a definite loss if the price is increased beyond an optimal range.

Diagram A shows the growth in the economy of the Middle East Region, Diagram B the accumulated outside wealth of the same region as functions of the oil price, given in relative terms. The existence of an optimal price from the viewpoint of the exporting region is quite apparent.

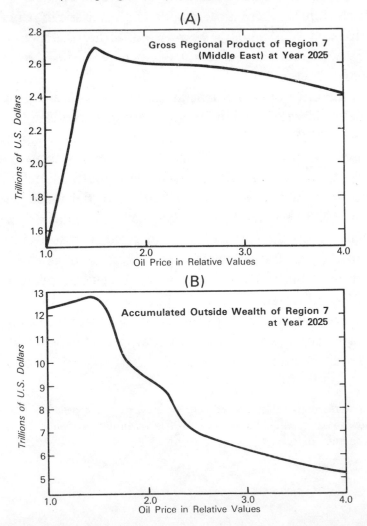

increases fourfold, the 2025 GRP in Region 7 falls back to $2.4 trillion.

Another criterion that can be used in considering oil price increases is the wealth which the Region 7 can accumulate during the 50-year period, by using excess oil revenues. Had the price of oil remained constant at the initial level, sales would have been quite high, and the Middle East would have been able to acquire considerable capital abroad. In the scenarios with higher maximal oil prices, the accumulated wealth increases but only in the scenarios where the maximal price is up to around 50 percent higher than the initial oil price (Fig. 7–1B). Here again, if the price rises too much, demand will taper off. If the price increases twofold the potential for accumulated outside wealth comes to less than one half of the value attainable in the scenario best for the Region 7.

The message of these studies apparently is that the sky is not the limit for increases in the price of oil. To achieve maximum growth and maximum accumulated wealth, the Middle East should arrive at a "most beneficial" price for oil somewhere around 50 percent greater than the initial price. Obviously the price cannot be increased that much in one step—that would have the same effect as too great an overall increase and would reduce demand. So the next question for the Region 7 exporters is over what time span the increases should be made, and when should the "most beneficial"—from the Middle East's own viewpoint—price be reached? Then, there is the question of how the optimal price depends on various factors which determine oil substitution. Analysis of all these questions shows that variations of the optimal price are comparatively small; the world system is not really seriously disrupted unless the optimal price range is ignored.

But what of the importing regions? How do they fare in the scenarios favorable to the exporters? Will these "beneficial" price increases dislocate or perhaps even ruin their economies?

Finally, can the conflict be viewed from both regions' sides—exporting and importing—in order to assess how they both fare under different scenarios? Two kinds of answers could result from such an assessment:

1. It might appear that there are some scenarios that strongly favor one of the two sides. The world system would then be facing an intrinsic conflict (for the resolution of which there would have to be some extraneous considerations).

2. The conflict might appear to be of such a nature that there exist some scenarios that are preferable for all concerned—that is, are optimal for exporting and importing regions. If either side deviates from the conditions specified by these scenarios, it would lose in comparison to what it could maximally gain otherwise. The only motivation to deviate from what appears to be an optimal scenario would be a negative one—that is, the expectation that the other side would lose even more. However, if the motivation for all participants is positive—that is, each is concerned only with its own maximal gains—there exists a ground for rational conflict resolution.

In order to study the possibility of such a rational resolution, we aggregated our regions into four groups: (1) the Developed World consisting of North America, Western Europe, Japan and Rest of Developed (Regions 1, 2, 3, and 4); (2) the Socialist World comprised of USSR, Eastern Europe and China (Regions 5 and 10); (3) the Middle East (Region 7); (4) the Rest of the Developing Regions

(Regions 6, 8, and 9). As the basis for our evaluation we have taken the gross regional product achieved in the year 2025 by each of the aggregated regions. The results of the analysis can best be represented in terms of two scenarios (Fig. 7–2).

In the *first low price scenario*—it is assumed that the oil price remains at the level of the early 1970s: $1.35 per barrel in 1963 prices. The world system model indicates that such an extremely low level of oil prices would hinder the development of alternative resources until the total world oil reserves are almost completely exhausted around the year 2000. Somewhat surprisingly, the most seriously affected region would be the Developed World, which initially had benefited most from the low oil prices and which, if pursuing always the short-term objectives, would never favor an increase in oil price. The Developed World would have to face a decline around the year 2010, followed by a recovery toward the end of the period, reaching a gross regional product level of "only" $5.5 trillion in 2025. The Middle East and Less Developed Regions fare rather poorly, the former reaching only a little over $300 billion in gross regional product by 2025, with stagnation in the second decade of the next century due to depletion of its major resource, oil. Actually, the situation appears much more dramatic if the regions which constitute the Developed World aggregate are examined separately. For example, North America is much less affected by the depletion of the oil resources in the Middle East than are Western Europe and Japan: If the total Developed World were to have a 1 percent annual decline due to oil shortage, Western Europe would have a 3 percent annual decline and Japan even more. Were that condition to persist over a five-year period, the social pressures

and massive unemployment accompanying such a development would be hard to bear for the societies where the population is accustomed to a high material living standard.
Political consequences would most probably lead to a strong
pressure to change the social arrangements that constitute
the prevailing system, with unpredictable consequences.

In fact the price of oil could not have remained at the
low level of the early 1970s. The Middle East could not
have permitted the only source of income needed for its
development to be depleted; therefore the price would have
to go up to slow the outflow of oil. And the later that increase takes place, and the smaller the reserves at the time,
the steeper and more disastrous the increase would have
to be.

An increase in price, according to traditional wisdom, is
generally presumed to hurt the consumer—in this case the
oil-importing regions. To see whether, in the long run, this
is necessarily the case, we designed the second, or *"optimal
price" scenario,* in which we assume that the price of oil
follows a 3 percent annual increase until it reaches
the optimal level determined in earlier analyses. Using
vastly increased oil revenues, the Middle East reaches a
gross regional product of almost $2.5 trillion (more than
five times the GRP of the first scenario) in 2025. The rest
of the Developing World reaches a combined GRP of more
than $4 trillion (compared with less than $2 trillion in the
first scenario). The Socialist World also fares better in the
second scenario, reaching a 2025 GRP of $6.3 trillion.

But the most surprising is the performance of the Developed World. In spite of considerably higher oil prices,
the economic level reached at 2025 is higher in the second
than in the first scenario, reaching close to $8 trillion.

In other words, the higher prices paid by the principal consumer turned out to have been beneficial also to that consumer—a seemingly counter-intuitive conclusion. In the closer analysis, however, this makes perfect sense. The economies of the Developed World would have been significantly dislocated by the exhaustion of the oil reserves projected for 2010—exhaustion stimulated by the Developed World's heavy usage of oil at low prices. The higher prices, moreover, will force the Developed World to introduce alternative energy sources. The growth of the Developed World is also much steadier in the second scenario, although some leveling in the economic output around 2000 occurs due to depletion of *some* oil reserves.

In conclusion, then, the oil price of the early 1970s, though based on immediate production costs, was at an unhealthy low level. Because of it, economic growth in the Developed World—especially in Japan and Western Europe —was fueled at a rate that could not have been sustained over a long period of time. A continuation of this state of affairs would have led to either the stoppage or decline of economic growth in the Developed World; or, if that could have been avoided, it would have produced a fundamental change in the Developed World's economic system. Economies would have been controlled by directives rather than by prevailing market mechanisms.

The most important conclusion that can be drawn from our analysis of the oil situation is this: the conflict between the two sides in the dilemma over finite resources is more apparent than real. In the long run, when all important factors are accounted for and the long-range benefits considered, cooperation is the only sensible and the most beneficial path for all participants. Attempts by one side to take

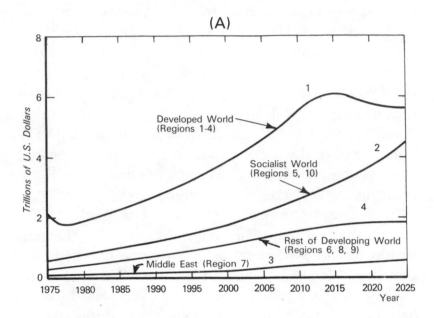

Cheap energy in the form of oil has been a prime fuel for the unprecedented growth of the world economy in the 1950's and 1960's. The dramatic increase in oil prices in 1973 was viewed as a catastrophe. However, computer analysis of our world system model indicates that the continuation of what amounts to overexploitation of oil, spurred by an unreasonably low price, would lead to major dislocations because of the exhaustion of reserves and the lack of motivation to develop substitutes in time. Pursuance of short term objectives would lead to major dislocations in the long run (see A). A much more beneficial development for all concerned results from the 'optimal price scenario' in which the price is gradually increased

(B)

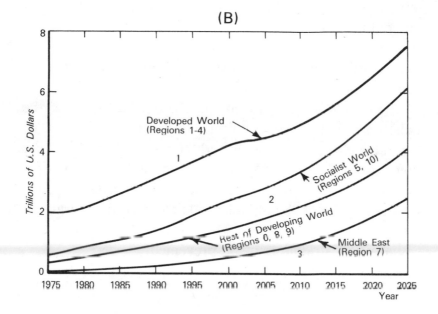

up to the 'optimum' level. Such a policy would bring in the
substitutes in a more regular fashion while prolonging the reserves. Both exporting and importing regions would fare better
(see B). It is only by taking a global and long term view that
such a course of development, most beneficial to all concerned,
can be identified.

significant advantage over the other backfire; they reduce the benefits to all.

This conclusion, of course, refers to the long run. Short-term advantages gained by quick, one-sided action will not only prove not to be advantageous; they will make solutions more elusive later. The real solution to the resources dilemma must be based on global and long-range considerations.

The conclusion applies not just to oil, but to all of the finite resources—food, fertilizer, copper, and so forth. The "most beneficial" price range and the proper rate of increase differ for each commodity, but the optimal level exists for all and should be determined and then on a global basis maintained worldwide by all participants in the world system—if recurrence of the world economic crises due to resources-constraints is to be prevented.

CHAPTER 8

Limits to Independence

As competition persists and conflicts deepen, confrontation between protagonists moves from the level of a mere "quarrel" to that of a "fight." The normal economic measures to resolve conflicts are no longer sufficient, and measures of retaliation have to be used. Will such an escalation lead to a decisive advantage for one of the combatants?

To analyze such a worsened situation, we shall continue to use the worldwide oil crisis as our example. It stands repeating, however, that in this new age of scarcity, what is true of energy is also true of other finite resources. If we can further bolster the thesis that global, interregional cooperation is the only sound means for dealing with prospective energy shortages, we are of course implying that cooperation is the only sound means for approaching other shortages too.

In the preceding chapter we concentrated mostly on pricing as the mechanism by which potential conflicts between oil producers and consumers could be averted or resolved. In the reality of the modern world, however, the pricing mechanism is but one of the moving parts that regulate the flow of oil. During the Arab oil embargo, the pricing mechanism was all but discarded as the oil producers applied supply restrictions; thus, the exporters intervened directly in the development processes of the importers. If such an adverse situation were extended, genuine shortages would emerge: on the one side there would be an energy shortage, and on the other a shortage of capital goods. No manipulation of prices could overcome these physical shortages. The economies of each of the regions affected by its shortage would have to slow down to adjust to the shortage; then various economic and political measures would have to be applied to stimulate the economies and eventually to restore conditions to the point where the shortages could be alleviated. In the world based on modern technology, the possibility of a region's learning to live with the shortage and to continue to develop is not very great; thus, the alleviation of shortages becomes a process of competitive bargaining, retaliation, and blackmail, all of which deepen the confrontation aspects of world system. The manipulation of the pricing mechanism for resolving conflicts generated by severe shortages of resources does not suffice. To find out what developments would take place if more restrictive measures are taken, we have analyzed a large number of scenarios, which we have grouped into three sets: the "squeeze" scenarios, the "retaliation" scenarios, and the "cooperation" scenarios.

For the sake of simplicity we shall restrict our findings to the two most directly affected world-region aggregates:

the Developed World (Regions 1 through 4) and the Middle East (Region 7). The performance indicator of the Developed World will be the gross regional product attained in the year 2025. The performance indicator for the Middle East will be the gross regional product in 2025 plus the outside wealth accumulated by that year.

The principal options that the Middle East can exercise in its competition with the Developed World are price changes and production regulation. The options for the Developed World include a set of "peaceful" measures— such as the development of alternative energy sources and a reduction in oil consumption—as well as "retaliatory" measures—such as raising the prices and taxes of export goods needed in the Middle East to correspond to increases in the price of imported oil.

In the *first*, or *"squeeze,"* scenario, we assume that the oil exporters are withholding the supply of oil, as they did late in 1973 (Fig. 8–1). The oil embargo of that year, however, was to a significant extent politically motivated in order to achieve a temporary objective. In the first scenario we take the view that constraints on production are introduced as a matter of long-term economic policy aimed at securing maximum economic gain in absolute terms. In other words, we assume that production constraints are used for the long-term benefit of the producing region.

But in the first scenario production constraints are not applied immediately. Eventually, they must be applied, lest the Middle East deplete all of its reserves, which would not, of course, be in the best interests of the region. But in the first stages of the scenario, the Middle East does supply what the world demands from it in oil. Profiting from the optimal price policy (a 3 percent annual price rise until the optimal price level of about 50 percent greater than the initial price is attained), the Middle East receives a flow of capital sufficient to ensure regional economic growth; the region also is able to secure a "healthy" accumulation of foreign capital. When the annual demand reaches 14 billions barrels,* production level is kept constant, since a further increase would rapidly deplete the remaining oil reserves. At this point, according to our computer analysis, a real oil shortage develops and persists until the user's technology makes adjustments (such as the development of mass transportation systems) to compensate for the shortage, and until new energy sources (nuclear, coal gasification, geothermal, solar, etc.) can be introduced. While the Middle East proceeds on an apparently regular path of growth, the Developed World is hit badly.

The Developed World suffers because its economy, which adapts to steady increases in prices rather well, responds very poorly to a sudden reduction in physical inputs, especially energy resources. When a physical shortage persists, a relatively long period of little or no growth occurs until a balance is restored, or the shortage is compensated for by other developments. If the Middle East cuts off its oil production at 14 billion barrels per year, the gross regional product of the Developed World would reach "only" $7 trillion at the end of the 1975–2025 period. At the same time the Middle East will achieve a respectable GRP of $1.8 trillion—almost the same as it would be without a produc-

---

* This production restriction is relatively mild. Without restriction Middle East oil production would, according to our analysis, reach about 17 billion barrels per year in 2015. Thereafter, though, it would rise quickly, reaching nearly 25 billion barrels in 2025.

tion ceiling. Of course, the sluggishness of the Developed World's economy will cause the Middle East to lose much of its accumulated wealth, but the larger amounts of oil remaining in the ground must be considered a compensating factor.

The *first scenario* (Fig. 8–1) assumes that the Developed World adjusts to increased prices as well as to supply restrictions by purely internal mechanisms; it takes no initiatives, takes no preventative measures, makes no attempts to anticipate likely future developments in order to influence the course of events. In other words, the scenario assumes a purely passive response. Such behavior certainly is plausible; indeed, history is filled with such examples. Yet purely reactive measures are not the only possibility. Anticipatory actions must also be considered.

If the Developed World anticipates price increases and production constraints on the part of the Middle East, it may choose to apply retaliatory actions. The Developed World may try to become self-sufficient in energy resources. Or, it may increase the cost of exports—of capital goods in particular—in proportion to the increased price and controlled supply of oil. We have analyzed a number of "retaliatory" scenarios with our computer model. Under conditions prevailing in these scenarios, the oil shortage would not last. At least in the immediate future, the Developed World probably could—at enormous expense—provide for its oil needs with regional sources. The increase in the cost of capital goods coupled with the oil price rise would slow down the economic development of the Middle East and cut drastically into that region's accumulated wealth. In typical *retaliatory scenarios* (Fig. 8–2), the Middle East would lag only slightly in economic development—reaching $1.6 tril-

Figure 8-1 Analysis of World Oil Situation and Its Economic Impact — Scenario 1

The principal characteristic of this scenario is a withholding of oil production by the Middle East Region according to a schedule that includes a ceiling at about 14 billion barrels per year. Graph A shows how the price of oil is assumed to change, reaching an "optimal" level in a 3 percent annual increase, and how the portion of energy demand covered by oil changes over the years; the total oil world trade and world oil deficit as determined by the model is also shown. Graph B shows how some important oil-producing regions share in the world production. Graph C shows the gross regional product achieved by the two main protagonists: Region A (Developed World Regions 1, 2, 3, and 4 aggregated) shown by Curve 1 and Region 7 shown by Curve 2. Curves 3 and 4 indicate the portion of the total capital in the developed world which could be acquired by Region 7 under two extreme assumptions regarding the management of excess oil revenues.

The scenario indicates a steady economic growth of Region 7 but a setback for Region A as a result of "oil squeeze" at different times.

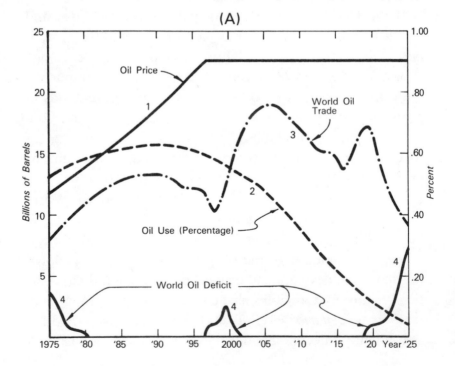

(A)

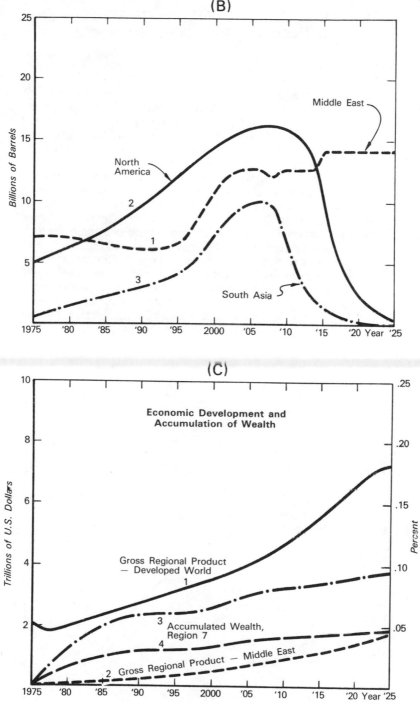

(B)

North America

Middle East

South Asia

(C)

Economic Development and Accumulation of Wealth

Gross Regional Product — Developed World

Accumulated Wealth, Region 7

Gross Regional Product — Middle East

Figure 8-2 Analysis of World Oil Situation and Its Economic Impact — Scenario 2

The principal characteristic of this scenario is "retaliation" by the Developed World Region against oil price increases imposed by the Middle East Region in the sense that the increase in the cost of export of investment goods is linked with the increase in oil cost. Graph A gives the price of oil, which is assumed to reach an "optimal" level in a 3 percent increase, and the portion of energy demand covered by oil together with the total oil world trade and world deficit in oil as determined by the model. Graph B shows how some important oil-producing regions share in the world production. Graph C shows the gross regional product achieved by the two main protogonists: the Developed World Region, shown by Curve 1, and the Middle East Region shown by Curve 2. Curves 3 and 4 indicate the portion of the total capital in the developed world which could be acquired by the Middle East under two extreme assumptions regarding the management of excess oil revenues.

The scenario shows that the wealth accumulated by the Middle East Region will be much less than in Scenario 1.

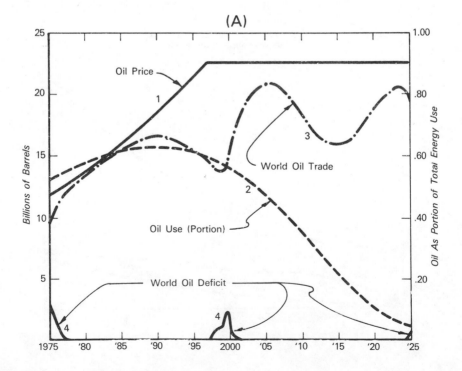

(A)

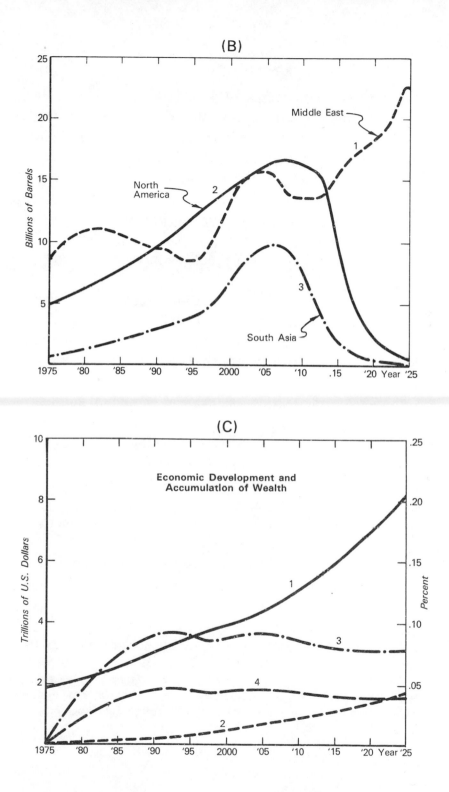

(B)

Billions of Barrels

25

20

Middle East

1

North
America

2

15

10

3

South Asia

5

1975   '80   '85   '90   '95   2000   '05   '10   '15   '20 Year '25

(C)

10

.25

Economic Development and
Accumulation of Wealth

Trillions of U.S. Dollars

8

.20

Percent

6

.15

1

4

.10

3

2

4

.05

2

1975   '80   '85   '90   '95   2000   '05   '10   '15   '20 Year '25

lion level by 2025, compared with $1.8 trillion in the first scenario—but the reduction in the Middle East's accumulated wealth would decline below $1 trillion.* The Developed World, faring much better than in the "squeeze" scenarios, would surpass the $8 trillion GRP level by 2025. In fact, it is quite possible that the Middle East, subjected to the retaliatory actions of the Developed World, would relax its production restrictions, thus, again, serving its short-term needs only, and exhausting its oil reserves rather quickly.

The alternative to these two conflict-scenarios, in which each side in turn attempts to take decisive advantage of the weakness of the other, is the *"cooperation" scenario* (Fig. 8–3). In order to assess what either side might have to sacrifice by cooperative action, we have specified a scenario with these characteristics: the price of oil and oil consumption as a percentage of total energy demand follow the same courses as in preceding cases. The optimal price increase level is retained. However, in the cooperation scenario, the Middle East does not resort to a production ceiling, but rather responds to the demand in correspondence with the optimal price level. The Developed World does not increase the cost of capital goods beyond the rise demanded by normal economic forces. The Developed World does not undertake a deliberate crash program to establish self-sufficiency in oil, although it does proceed at a normal pace to develop regional oil resources and alternative sources of energy. Finally, the Middle East reinvests all accumulated excess

* If the Middle East region resorts at the same time to "squeeze" by withholding production, the accumulated wealth would be even further reduced to $400 billion while the Developed World would reach only $7 trillion.

oil revenues in the Developed World: this not only prevents a further currency drain from the Developed World but it also establishes a real partnership between the economies of the oil-producing and oil-consuming regions.

The analysis of the cooperation scenario yields rather astonishing conclusions. The Developed World retains its relatively high level of growth as indicated in the retaliatory type scenarios: $8.2 trillion in 2025, while the Middle East preserves the advantages of the squeeze scenarios reaching $1.8 trillion and the accumulation of twice the outside capital as in some conflict scenarios (between 7 and 10 percent of the Developed World's capital by 2025).

Our computer analysis indicates, as before, *that global cooperation offers much better conditions than conflict for all concerned.* But, no computer can predict whether men will be rational enough to follow this path; however, the computer does give rational men all the evidence they need to convince other men that the emergence of a new world system is a matter of necessity, not preference, and that that system must be built on cooperation. Cooperation is no longer a schoolroom word suggesting an ethical but elusive mode of behavior; cooperation is a scientifically supportable, politically viable, and absolutely essential mode of behavior for the organic growth of the world system.

And cooperation, finally, requires that the people of all nations face up to an admission that may not come easy. Cooperation by definition connotes interdependence. Increasing interdependence between nations and regions must then translate as a decrease in independence. Nations cannot be interdependent without each of them giving up some of, or at least acknowledging limits to, its own independence.

In late 1973 a government spokesman declared, "We

Figure 8-3   Analysis of World Oil Situation and Its Economic Impact — Scenario 3

The principal characteristic of this scenario is cooperation. The flow of oil from the Middle East Region is unimpeded and the export-import between the regions is governed solely by the economic forces without undue interference from the political level. Graph A gives the price of oil, which is assumed to reach an "optimal" level in a 3 percent annual increase, and the portion of energy demand covered by oil, together with the total oil world trade and world deficit as determined by the model. Graph B shows how some important oil-producing regions share in the world production. Graph C shows the gross regional product achieved by the two main protagonists: the Developed World Region shown by Curve 1 and the Middle East Region shown by Curve 2. Curves 3 and 4 indicate the portion of the total capital in the developed world which could be acquired by the Middle East Region under two extreme assumptions regarding the management of excess oil revenues.

The scenario clearly shows the advantages of cooperation to the Middle East Region in terms of accumulated wealth and to the Developed World Region in terms of uninterrupted growth. Cooperaton is obviously a superior strategy for all concerned.

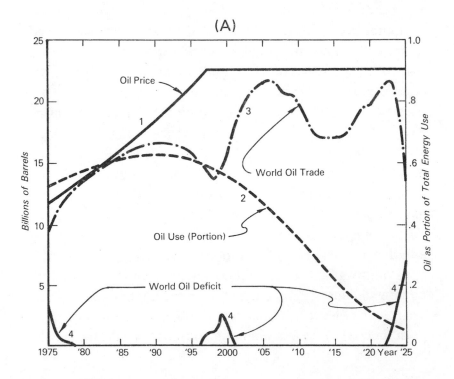

(A)

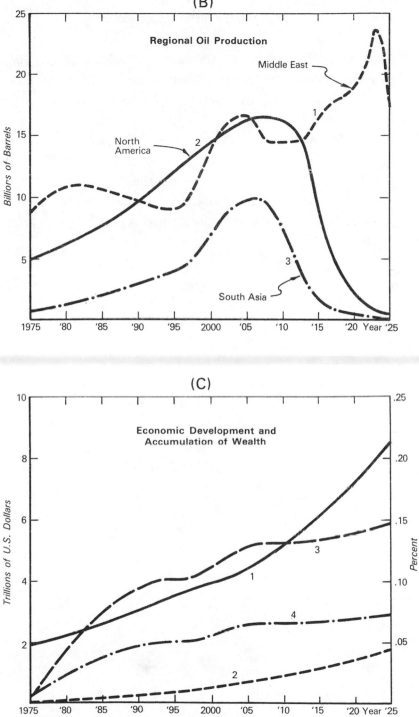

(B)

Regional Oil Production

Middle East

North America — 2

South Asia — 3

1

Billions of Barrels

1975 '80 '85 '90 '95 2000 '05 '10 '15 '20 Year '25

(C)

**Economic Development and
Accumulation of Wealth**

Trillions of U.S. Dollars

Percent

3

1

4

2

1975 '80 '85 '90 '95 2000 '05 '10 '15 '20 Year '25

shall bear all sacrifices to preserve our independence. Independence is our most sacred heritage in the very foundation of our nation." Was he referring to a former colony trying to liquidate the remnants of a colonial age, or to a small nation dominated economically and trying to stave off neocolonialism? No, the nation is one of the world's most powerful—the United States—and the statement acknowledged, even if unintentionally, *the dawn of an era of limits to independence—even for the strongest and biggest nations of the world.*

CHAPTER 9

The Only Feasible Solution

"Morally it makes no difference whether a man is killed in war or is condemned to starve to death by the indifference of others."
—Willy Brandt
before the United
Nations General
Assembly 1973

The most precious of all resources is food. Given even the most optimistic projections for population growth during the next fifty years, the worldwide demand for this resource will increase severalfold. But to grasp the seriousness of the food problem and to comprehend the strain the demand for food will impose on the world system, one does not have to look into the future at all: the situation is *already* critical. Here are several observations that illustrate the existing situation:

According to a UNESCO estimate, between 400 and 500 million children suffered from malnutrition and starvation in 1973. Ghastly as that figure is, it describes a state of affairs that is not new. It has been calculated that the availability of food per capita worldwide has not increased since 1936 and actually decreased in the last decade.*

* M. Guernier, "Perspectives alimentaires de l'an 2000," personal report to the Club of Rome, 1974.

Ten years ago, world food stockpiles for emergency re-
lief amounted to an eighty-day supply. Today those reserves
are sufficient for only thirty days' consumption—a nearly
threefold reduction.*

Before World War II, the world was about evenly divided into regions that imported food and regions capable
of exporting food. Since the war, some regions—most significantly Latin America and Eastern Europe—that were
exporters have become importers. Moreover, according to
present estimates, only North America and Australia realistically can be considered major potential sources of food
supply.

The vital question is whether the precarious world food
situation is a temporary phenomenon—perhaps the result
of an oversight—or a persistent problem. If the latter is the
case, the urgent issue is to determine what alternative strategies are available with which to achieve a sustainable
solution.

We have analyzed the global food problem with our
world model, and our analysis indicates that the historical
pattern of development will make the food supply situation
increasingly worse. And since the present situation is already producing catastrophic crises (as current developments in South Asia and Africa demonstrate), any further
aggravation of the problem can only be regarded as apo-
calyptic.

In order to determine a suitable strategy to deal with
the problem, we have investigated a number of alternatives.
From all of the scenarios we were able to distill some basic

* L. Brown, "An Exchange on Food," Foreign Policy Association Report No. 14, 1974.

ingredients that must be incorporated into any strategy aimed at the solution of the world food crisis. Before presenting our conclusions, however, we should point out some of the specific features of our world model relevant to the problem of world food supply.

The diets of the people in various parts of the world differ, depending, of course, on the availability and type of food in the various regions, and on climate and even cultural factors. Our model is region-specific in terms of diet which is described in reference to twenty-six different types of foods. The model also evaluates the importance of *lack* of essential diet components (such as protein) on the various populations. Although we are dealing with a "world food problem," the regionalized structure of the model is significant because it allows us to analyze the relationship between the location of actual food supplies and the location of actual food and nutrition deficiencies. For example, there may be a great potential for increasing the production of prime beef in Latin America, so much so that Latin America could become one of the world's leading exporters of this major source of protein. South Asia is protein-poor. Now if we were dealing in raw statistics or on a non-selective worldwide basis —that is, if we had not used a comprehensive computer model, or if we had viewed the world as a homogeneous system—we might conclude that Latin America's ability to produce protein-rich food could somehow be applied to bolstering the diet of protein-poor South Asia. Needless to say, Latin America's protein is virtually useless in South Asia, where diets do not include beef. Thus, regionalization of the food problem is a prerequisite for any realistic treatment.

Our model also permits a comprehensive approach—

that is, an approach based on study at every level of the world system. Too often the question of world food supply is considered solely within the confines of economics. In that context it has been stated that all we need is a 3 percent annual increase in the agricultural output of the world economy to feed the population. However, one does not eat dollars but grains; the real question is how much food can actually be physically produced. Nor can a laboratory approach solve problems since the problem is not what a "wizard" could do, if he could transform all arable land in the world into a greenhouse. We need rather to determine what can be produced with land of the type and amount available and with existing economic and human resources. We know, for example, what can be done with fertilizer (Fig. 9–1), but as we have mentioned previously in this report, the availability of fertilizer is affected by such seemingly unrelated phenomena as pleasure-driving in the Developed World. In short, one has to look comprehensively and carefully into the entire world system. Assessing the development of the world food supply on the basis of laboratory or experimental results leads to rather naive, if not downright irresponsible, conclusions. After all, human lives deserve better than cavalier treatment. Hence, the laboratory approach is also fully inadequate.

The conflicts which might arise from the finiteness of the world food supply are deeper than the conflicts considered in earlier chapters. It is truly a struggle for survival. The resolution of the conflicts cannot be limited to economic means (as was the case in less serious situations considered in the preceding chapters), but must involve all aspects of social and individual behavior.

The most critical gap between food need and food supply

Brief on Increase in Agricultural Yield

Increase in the agricultural production of a given amount of
arable land depends on two types of factors: 1. use of technological inputs such as fertilizers, improved seeds, pesticides,
etc.; 2. increase in agricultural capital, resulting in improved
mechanization, irrigation, infrastructure, etc. To represent this
complex relationship we have used a family of curves (see A).
For a given capitalization the yield increases on a diminishing
return to scale curve as the technological input increases; as
the capitalization changes the yield-technological input curve
changes. The heavy line in A shows an example of the increase in yield as a result of a policy of increased capitalization and increased technological input.

   The historical data for South and Southeast Asia giving the
increase in yield achieved over the last two decades and the
corresponding use of fertilizer is shown in B.

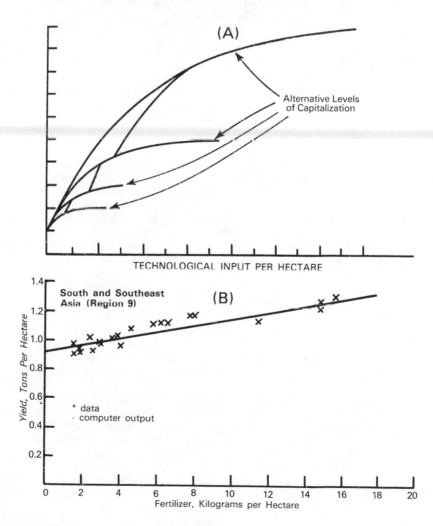

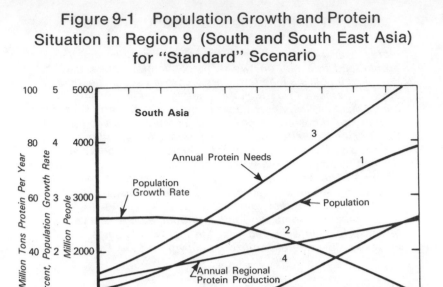

Figure 9-1 Population Growth and Protein Situation in Region 9 (South and South East Asia) for "Standard" Scenario

The "Standard" Scenario is based on the assumption that a population policy is initiated that leads in about fifty years to equilibrium fertility. Thereby, the population grows from 1.3 billion in 1975 to 3.8 billion in 2025 (Curve 1) while the growth rate of this region declines from a little over 2.5 to 1 percent (Curve 2). It is furthermore assumed that the population is adequately fed, and thus no starvation would slow down the population growth. Then the protein needs (Curve 3) of South Asia would increasingly surpass her own protein production (Curve 4) so that at the end of the fifty-year period considered, the protein deficit (Curve 5) is larger than her own estimated protein production of around 50 million tons. The grain import necessary to cover this protein deficit (due to the fact that more than 90 percent of all the protein consumed in South Asia is of vegetable origin this is also a calorie deficit) would increase to about a half billion tons annually by 2025 and would continue to grow. This amount is twice the present North American grain crop, and even if it were available for export to South Asia, it would pose practically insurmountable transportation and distribution problems. The increase of the regional production in South Asia is based on making all potentially arable land available for cultivation and on achieving a steadily rising yield per hectare. These production levels assume productivity comparable to that achieved by introduction of improved grains — the "Green Revolution" — on the best irrigated land in India, which is probably an overly optimistic assumption.

exists today in South Asia and Tropical Africa. Because of
the sheer numbers of people affected, the problem is greatest
in South Asia, and we shall illustrate our findings in reference to that region. Our conclusions, however, are applica-
ble to Tropical Africa and to any other needy region.

The purpose of the *first,* or *standard, scenario* is to provide a clue to the persistency of the food deficiency problem
during the next fifty years. The scenario assumes that the
historical pattern of development based on a somewhat optimistic view of the past and present situation will continue.
As before, this optimism is reflected in our population estimates. We again assume that an equilibrium fertility level
will be attained in about fifty years. We also assume,
quite optimistically, that the average use of fertilizer per
hectare in the entire region will surpass the present North
American level toward the end of the fifty-year period. At
that time South Asia alone will consume more fertilizer
than the whole world consumed in 1960. Assuming that
the fertilizer is used on every piece of land under cultivation,
the yield per hectare will increase by about 1000 kilograms
—approximately the increase that the Green Revolution
brought to the best lands in India and Pakistan in recent
years, before the supply of fertilizer began to dwindle. Still
proceeding optimistically, we assume that all remaining
arable land in South Asia is quickly brought under cultivation, and that all technological inputs, such as irrigation
systems (which must accompany the fertilizer to produce
high-yielding grain), will be available as needed. Finally,
we have assumed that no mass starvation takes place. The
difference between the food needs of the region and the
food production in the region dictates the quantity of food
that must be imported and is assumed to have been made
available by other regions.

Because protein deficiency is already the most serious aspect of the present food supply situation, we have focused our attention on the total protein content of the food available or needed. In more than half the world, the protein content of the average diet is about two thirds of the daily need, and the consumption of animal protein is hardly one-fourth the required.* Furthermore, since the food supply in South Asia is primarily grain, there is a close relationship between protein and caloric intake. If one is low, so is the other.

Our computer analysis, pregnant with optimism, shows clearly that the food crisis in South Asia will worsen. In spite of all the advancements assumed, the availability of fertilizer and land assumed, the lack of intervening disaster assumed, the protein deficit will continuously increase; by the year 2025 it will be up to 50 million tons annually. Such deficits could never be closed by imports: to pay for that quantity of imports, South Asia would have to spend one third of its total economic output, and three times what it earns from exports. But even if South Asia had that kind of money, the physical problems of handling those quantities of food would be incredible. In one year the region would then have to import 500 million tons of grain—*twice as much as the total tonnage of all goods now being shipped overseas from the United States.* And that is assuming that that quantity of grain would be grown for export elsewhere—500 million tons, after all, is larger than the total grain production of the entire Developed World. Moreover, these quantities would have to be delivered every year, in ever increasing amounts, without end. In sum, it would be impossible.

* See Alexi Pokrovsky in *Ceres,* November–December 1972.

But what would happen if those imports were not available? That question forms the basis of our *second,* or *"tragic,"* scenario. All of our optimistic assumptions have remained, except that we assume that importation of grain will not be part of the picture. The catastrophe would start in the early 1980s and peak around 2010: deaths related to the food shortage would be double the normal death rate.* Thereafter, the death rate will decline, but only because the earlier deaths reduced the birth rate for a later generation. Or, to put it more cruelly but simply, the people who would be having babies died when they were babies. The number of food-related deaths in the fifty-year period ending in 2025 would be, in the age 0–15 group alone, about 500 million children. With the death rate increased to equal the birth rate, as in medieval times, an equilibrium population actually would be restored eventually, but clearly this is no way to achieve that end; there is indeed no reason to assume that the affected peoples would stand for it. In such a situation starvation would extend its strangling hold over vast regions inhabited by hundreds of millions of people. The population would appear to be trapped, since there would be no fertile areas to go to (as the present events in Africa have shown); vast populations would slowly deteriorate. There is no historical precedent for this kind of slow destruction—the massive, agonizing reduction of the population of an entire world region once inhabited by several billion people!

In the *third scenario* we investigated the possibility that the region could become self-sufficient in food by 2025. To achieve this, regional investment would be shifted from in-

* See Appendix III (E) on "Starvation and Mortality."

Figure 9-2 Effect of Actual Food Deficit

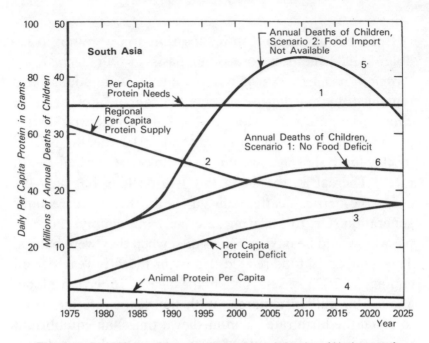

The graph depicts with a horizontal straight line (1) the total daily protein needs per person of seventy grams, and by Curve 2 the daily regional per capita protein supply (vegetable plus very low animal protein, see Curve 4), and the daily per capita protein deficit, Curve 3, that would exist if South Asia's population were to grow (without starvation-induced higher mortality) from 1.3 to 3.8 billion. If the imports needed to cover this protein deficit were not forthcoming, starvation would take a heavy toll, particularly among children. Curve 5 shows the number of annual child deaths to be expected then (population would grow only to about 3 billion), and Curve 6 the annual number of deaths of children, if sufficient food were provided through imports. About the mid-1980s Curve 5 begins to rise steeply over Curve 6. The decline in the number of child deaths from 2010 exists because, with the exceedingly large number of child deaths after 1985, the age structure of the population is changed so that the children's portion of the total population has drastically diminished, leading, with a fifteen to twenty year delay, to a considerable decrease in the number of fertile women. The total aggregate number of additional child deaths up to the year 2025 amounts to more than a half billion. Of course, these figures should not be taken as forecasts; they are given solely to provide the reader with a well-considered estimate of the order of magnitude of human suffering which is in store for South Asia if the problems of population growth and food supply are not solved.

dustry to agriculture; virtually all monies now being spent for industrial development would be invested in farming. The computer analysis shows that the grain yield per hectare would rise initially more quickly than under normal conditions, reach a peak around the turn of the century, then decline. By 2025 the grain production of the region would not be larger than it would have been without the shift in capital from industry to agriculture. For without an industrial base, the region's economy would be eroded; unemployment would rise to unmanageable proportions; and social and political chaos would wreck the fabric of the region long before 2025.

For our fourth scenario we returned to a population policy to see if a more effective one could help make the food picture for South Asia less bleak. In this scenario we assumed that an equilibrium fertility rate is achieved in only fifteen years. Special attention is given to agriculture, but not so much that the industrial sector is destroyed. The analysis indicates that malnutrition could not be avoided without importation of food. Imports would not be so unmanageably great as in the earlier scenarios, however, and would not become essential until later in the period. The imports would amount to about one fifth the requirements of the first scenario. The cost of importing so much food would still be prohibitive. But at least the problem has, at last, been reduced to economics.

In the *fifth scenario,* investment aid is provided to South Asia in sufficient amount and at the time needed to close the food-supply gap and the export-import imbalance. The magnitude of such a program will require a concerted effort by the entire Developed World. The export potential of South Asia would be increased substantially, and the world

Figure 9-3 Economic Indicators for South Asia

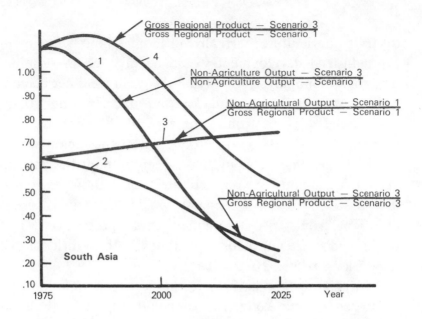

In view of the huge food deficit in South Asia it was proposed to shift investment and working capital away from the non-agricultural to the agricultural sector in order to achieve a higher degree of self-sufficiency in food. Curve 1, which gives the ratio of nonagricultural output of the economy in Scenario 3 and Scenario 1 (Standard scenario), depicts vividly the complete collapse of the nonagricultural sector in such a case. Also the total gross regional product (GRP) of Region 9, though it benefits (see Curve 4) during the first fifteen years from the increase in agricultural production caused by the investment shift, drops finally to about 10 percent of its "normal" amount in 2025. Agricultural production just cannot sustain its quick early growth because of the increasing weakness of the non-agricultural sector, which has to supply fertilizer, farm machinery, and infrastructure to agriculture. Hence, in the end (in 2025) agricultural production has not risen above the level it attained by then without the investment shift (see Curve 1). Curves 2 and 3 serve to confirm that with "normal" investment distribution (Curve 3) the nonagricultural portion of the GRP rises steadily to nearly two-thirds of the GRP, a necessary development in view of the faster-growing urban population, while the investment shift to the agricultural sector depresses the nonagricultural sector (Curve 2) to a completely unacceptable low level. Other proportions of the investment shift were examined, all leading to similar disastrous results, as soon as an effort was made to achieve a substantial increase in food production in the first ten to twenty years.

economic system would have to be modified so that South Asia could pay from exports for most of its food imports. These exports would have to be industrial, since the regional food demands obviously will absorb the local agricultural output. But to make this scenario feasible, the Developed World must help South Asia to develop its own exportable and competitive industrial specialization.

Scenario five—the only way to avert unprecedented disaster in South Asia—requires the emergence of a new global economic order. Industrial diversification will have to be worldwide and carefully planned with special regard for regional specificity. The most effective use of labor and capital, and the availability of resources, will have to be assessed on a global, long-term basis. Such a system cannot be left to the mercy of narrow national interests, but must rely on long-range world economic arrangements.

In summary, the only feasible solution to the world food situation requires:

1. A global approach to the problem.

2. Investment aid rather than commodity aid, except for food.

3. A balanced economic development for all regions.

4. An effective population policy.

5. Worldwide diversification of industry, leading to a truly global economic system.

Only a proper combination of these measures can lead to a solution. Omission of any one measure will surely lead to disaster. But the strains on the global food production capacity would be lessened if the eating habits in the affluent part of the world would change, becoming less wasteful.

The situation is more than urgent. Even our "solution" requires drastic, unprecedented changes in the world system.

Figure 9-4 Deadly Consequences
of Population Delay in South Asia

If a population control policy aimed at population equilibrium were to be initiated in South and Southeast Asia in 1990, it would result in a population development as depicted by Curve 1, leading to an increase of about 1.4 billion people in fifty years. If the same policy were started five years later, in 1995, the population growth (Curve 2) would be practically identical, also leading to about 3 billion inhabitants in South Asia in 2025. However, as far as mortality is concerned, particularly among children, the five year delay has — literally — deadly consequences (compare Curves 3 and 4). The number of additional child deaths caused by the five year delay would amount to more than 150 million, and more than a half billion additional child deaths would be avoided if the same population control policy were initiated in 1975. Early options available would be lost by unnecessary delay in taking determined action.

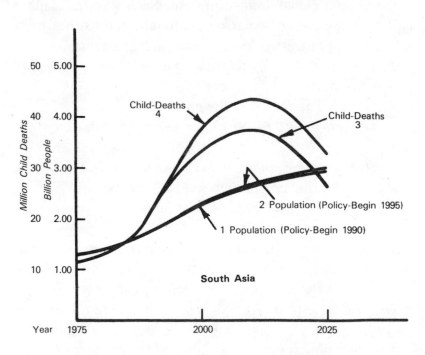

These changes cannot be effected without compromise on the part of the other regions. Even if there is willingness to work toward a solution, such compromises require a lot of time. In this case there is no time. Our analysis shows that if the population policy is less stringent and the transition period is extended from fifteen to thirty-five years, the number of accumulated child deaths in the fifty-year period will increase by 80 percent. If we wait twenty years to implement a policy with a transition period of 15 years,* there will be, between 1975 and 2025, an increase in child deaths of 300 percent!

The most thorough analyses of a large number of scenarios using our world system computer model lead to the inescapable conclusion that mankind's options for avoiding catastrophe are decreasing, while delays in implementing the options are, quite literally, deadly.

* This is a truly stunning difference, although both population policies lead in the year 2010 to an equilibrium fertility rate.

CHAPTER 10

Faustian Bargain: The Ultimate Technological Fix

The human race is getting to be too much for itself and too much for the world.
— *William Saroyan*

There are many views on the current energy crisis. On one hand it is argued that the energy crisis is "merely" a technological problem surely to be solved by yet another of the technological "fixes" which have always worked wonders; on the other hand the energy crisis is considered as a prelude to deep societal problems whose solution will require not only institutional and social changes but also a change in the very life-style of individuals and the relationship of man with nature.

There is little doubt that we are at present deeply immersed in a global energy crisis that will become worse before getting any better. It has become equally apparent that the solution to that crisis must be long term, governed by anticipatory thinking; the sheer size of the new technological edifice to be constructed will not allow an easy dismantling and a quick change in a new direction if a solution

130

selected on short-range considerations proves inadequate. The current decisions regarding which option is taken for the solution of the energy crises are therefore most important since we will have to live with the consequences of these decisions for some time to come. Extra careful planning and an explicit recognition of all kinds of costs and risks involved must therefore be undertaken.

A technological optimist's view holds that the solution of the energy crisis will ultimately be found in nuclear energy.

In twenty-five years, nuclear fission could carry 30 percent of the energy load of the Developed World (Regions 1, 2, 3, and 4), which means that nuclear energy then will approximate today's total energy requirements in these industrialized regions. In the short run, liquid fuel must be reserved for transportation and must not be "wasted" for heating or other non-essential uses. Gas exploration must be intensified, and where discovery of gas falls short, coal should be gasified to fill the gap. While we are waiting for nuclear energy to bear the entire load, we should be able to engineer "secondary" extractions from "exhausted" oil wells and to exploit the potential of tar sands and oil shale. In fifty years or so, the combination of "fast-breeders" with high-temperature gas-cooled reactors and hydrogen technology should satisfy all of our energy needs; it will even provide liquid fuel for transportation. Thus, the energy crisis will create only a slight dent in our economic growth—a bit of temporary shifting from consumption to investment—but on the whole, economic growth, including a further increase in energy consumption, can continue.

The problem with this prescription is that it makes the solution of a societal problem based solely on isolated technology look like a panacea. However, a solution can be found only by considering the entire system—all aspects of our world model, from environment to individual values and attitudes. Even now our technological edifices are gigantic; they do not lend themselves to easy dismantling and change. Perhaps, somewhere, someone is developing an alternative source of energy; but unless he also invents a system to replace the supporting network designed to service and be serviced by this new source, his better source won't be better at all because it won't be feasible.

Assume, as the technology optimists want us to, that in one hundred years all primary energy will be nuclear. Following historical patterns, and assuming a not unlikely quadrupling of population, we will need, to satisfy world energy requirements, 3000 "nuclear parks" each consisting of, say, eight fast-breeder reactors. The eight reactors, working at 40 percent efficiency, will produce 40 million kilowatts of electricity collectively. Therefore, each of the 3000 nuclear parks will be converting primary nuclear power equivalent to 100 million kilowatts thermal. The largest nuclear reactors presently in operation convert about 1 million kilowatts (electric), but we will give progress the benefit of doubt and assume that our 24,000 worldwide reactors are capable of converting 5 million kilowatts each. In order to produce the world's energy in one hundred years, then, we will merely have to build, in each and every year between now and then, *four reactors per week*! And that figure does not take into account the lifespan of nuclear reactors. If our future nuclear reactors last an average of thirty years, we shall eventually have to build about *two reactors per day* simply to replace those that have worn out. The implications of such a development in the Developed World will be even more pronounced, as it is shown in the case of the United States in Fig. 10.1.

Figure 10-1   Energy Supply Distribution
for Nuclear Option Scenario

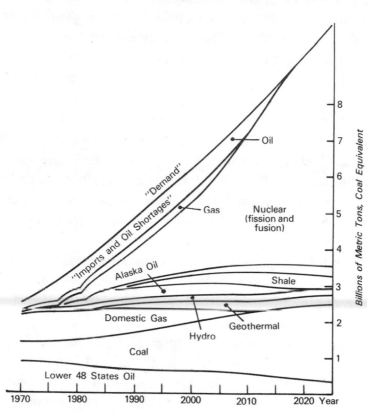

In the conditions of continued growth, it is important to look over a sufficiently long period of time in the future in order to assess the consequences of selecting one of the available alternatives. The graph in the figure gives projections made by the US Atomic Energy Commission of energy demands in the USA from 1975 up to the year 2000 and how this demand could be met if the decision is made in favor of relying on nuclear energy production. The full impact of such a decision can be seen only when the projection is extended over a sufficiently long period of time. By the year 2025 sole reliance on nuclear power would require more than 50 major nuclear installations, on the average, in every state of the union.

For the sake of this discussion, let us disregard whether this rate of construction is technically and organizationally feasible in view of the fact that, at present, the lead time for the construction of much smaller and simpler plants is seven to ten years. Let us also disregard the cost of about $2000 billion per year—or 60 percent of the total world output of $3400 billion—just to replace the worn-out reactors and the availability of the investment capital. We may as well also assume that we could find safe storage facilities for the discarded reactors and their irradiated accessory equipment, and also for the nuclear waste. Let us assume that technology has taken care of all these big problems, leaving us only a few trifles to deal with.

In order to operate 24,000 breeder reactors, we would need to process and transport, every year, 15 million kilograms of plutonium-239, the core material of the Hiroshima atom bomb. (Only ten pounds of the element are needed to construct a bomb.*) As long as it is not inhaled or otherwise introduced into the bloodstream of human beings, plutonium-239 can be safely handled without any significant radiological hazards. But if it is inhaled, ten micrograms [†] of plutonium-239 is likely to cause fatal lung cancer. A ball of plutonium the size of a grapefruit contains enough poison to kill nearly all the people living today. Moreover, plutonium-239 has a radioactive life of more than 24,000 years. Obviously, with so much plutonium on

---

* M. Willich and T. B. Taylor, *Nuclear Theft, Risks and Safeguards; A Report to the Energy Policy Project of The Ford Foundation* (Cambridge, Mass.: Ballinger Publishing Company, 1974).

† One microgram = one millionth of a gram.

hand, there will be a tremendous problem of safeguarding the nuclear parks—not one or two, but 3000 of them. And what about their location, national sovereignty, and jurisdiction? Can one country allow inadequate protection in a neighboring country, when the slightest mishap could poison adjacent lands and populations for thousands and thousands of years? And who is to decide what constitutes adequate protection, especially in the case of social turmoil, civil war, war between nations, or even only when a national leader comes down with a case of bad nerves. The lives of millions could easily be beholden to a single reckless and daring individual.

We need hardly belabor the point. A technological fix might very well become a Faustian bargain—and worse, for we would be selling not merely *our* soul to satisfy our immediate comfort needs, but the well-being and perhaps the very existence of *generations still unborn*. Most absurd, and ironic, however, is the fact that although the nuclear option is *not* the only option, and it is *not* inevitable, the Faustian bargain is being made almost unnoticed. In the process, other options are being foreclosed. It probably will develop that the nuclear option will not be completed: the barriers mentioned above would seem to be insurmountable, or not worth surmounting. But for not having tried any alternative, more feasible choices, the world may have to pay a terrible penalty.

The main attractiveness of the optimists' suggested solution to the energy crisis is that it is purely technological. But as we have consistently stressed, the problem itself is *not* purely technological. The problem is political, social, even psychological. The North American region, with only 6 percent of the world population, is presently consuming 30 percent of the world's energy. As shown by previous analyses with our model, the developed industrialized world is buying time to develop alternative sources of energy—buying time not by significantly reducing its consumption of energy, but by consuming in decades what took millions of years to form, and using global resources at the expense of less fortunate regions. As a result, the gap between "North" and "South" will be increasing, making it even less likely that the developing regions will ever catch up with what is referred to as the "developed" world. And the distance will be increased by using the resources from the regions that are being outpaced, since the dependence of the developed regions on essential resources from outside their own regions will increase considerably. Even if such a development were possible, by force or persuasion, is it desirable?

Can this aspect of the energy crisis have a technological solution? Does holding up the panacea of technology and asking people to have faith in its magical powers nourish the poor in India and in Africa? We have proven, by logical and factual analysis, that delay is deadly, that delay compounds crisis, that problems postponed are problems that may very well become insoluble, and yet we are asked to rely solely on technology to do the job sometime in the future.

However optimistic one might allow himself to be about the prospects for a rational approach to energy conservation over the next fifty years, one does have to admit, based on all available evidence, that energy demand will increase substantially. That being the case, alternative solutions to the Faustian bargain will have to be found.

We have used the regionalized world model to analyze a number of scenarios. A rather extensive analysis of historical trends in energy demand in all ten regions is used as a basis for alternative paths of future demands. (See Fig. 10.2.) Any scenario that seems to lead to a satisfactory solution to the energy crisis on the technological, economic, and socio-political levels must successfully combine three strategies in reference to the short, intermediate and long-term problems. The scenario which our analysis indicates as preferable is characterized by the following: The *short-range* strategy must ensure that enough oil flows from the oil-exporting regions to maintain the socio-economic stability of the oil-importing regions. In exchange for their cooperation, the oil producers are guaranteed a permanent role in the energy supply industry in the post-oil era. The *intermediate* strategy supplements primary energy sources with coal, gas, and liquefied coal. The *long-term* strategy is based on solar energy. In order to secure the cooperation of the oil-producing regions, and also to construct a balanced global economy, the necessary solar energy farms are built in the oil-producing regions. In this way the long-term strategy will keep the promise of the short-range strategy.

The short-range strategy refers to the coming decade; the intermediate strategy applies to the period between ten and twenty-five years in the future; and the long-term strategy should begin with the twenty-first century.

The advantage of maintaining a continuous flow of oil from the oil-producers to the oil-consumers in the immediate future should be obvious. Within the next ten years nuclear energy will contribute comparatively little to the solution of the energy crisis.

Coal, for all its limitations, is a reasonable temporary supplement to the world's energy resources in the period of transition: it is efficient, and there is plenty of it. At present,

Figure 10-2 Relationship Between Energy Demand and Economic Indicators as Derived from Historical Data

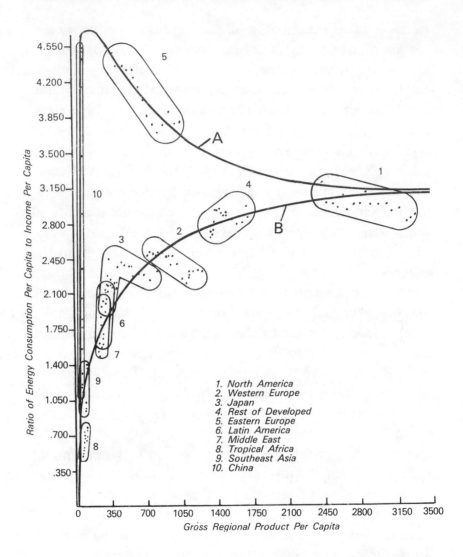

Energy demand depends on population, level of economic activity, and industrialization. Analysis of historical data for different regions indicates a relationship between the gross regional product per capita and the ratio of energy consumption per capita to income per capita. Two types of relationships are shown in the figure: for centrally planned economies, A — Regions 5 and 10; and for other regions, B. In Regions 5 and 10 the emphasis on heavy industry results in an early peak in energy consumption which, with the increase in the gross regional product per capita, seems to be approaching the relationship prevailing in other regions.

the total of known and identified coal reserves is more than 4500 billion tons worldwide. If the world population reaches and is maintained at, say, 10 billion (compared to 3.6 billion in 1970), and if the world's people can be persuaded to consume a per-capita average of about 4 kilowatts (thermal) in energy,* then the present stockpile of coal will last beyond the year 2100. The use of coal does present problems: its distribution is regionally peculiar; it is cumbersome and it does not burn as cleanly as oil and gas. But it is there, and it can be shipped, and it can even be made to burn cleaner (especially in its liquefied state). Moreover, its use for heating would extend the life of the world's oil reserves, and oil, freed of the dirty work, could lend itself to enterprises where it could do the most good: the making of fertilizer, synthetic fibers, protein, and so forth.

Inasmuch as one hundred years should be ample time for the development of all the necessary solar energy technology and hardware, nuclear energy—the technology optimists magical and dangerous solution—may never be needed. All things considered, solar energy is more satisfactory than nuclear energy. It is safer and cleaner, and might even be cheaper (when the waste-accumulation, social and political hazards, and environmental effects of nuclear energy are calculated), and its paraphernalia can be erected with impunity in even the most irresponsible domain. If the solar energy farms are built, at first, within the oil-producing regions, and jointly financed by the producers and the developed regions, the revenues from oil exportation would be reinvested in energy; the world monetary inflation would

* The average per-capita kilowatt consumption of energy in France today is 4; in the United States, however, the standard is 10 kw.

be helped, too, by this joint venture. Even more importantly, the energy-producing regions would remain energy-producing regions, even if and after their oil runs short. Thus would the economic stability of the world system be served leading also gradually to a limited worldwide decentralization of energy production.

To cover millions of acres with solar energy farms would constitute the most extensive engineering undertaking of all times. One percent of the world's land surface would probably be required, and the cost of the land, pipelines, and accessory equipment would probably cost between $20,000 and $50,000 billion. The total annual output of energy from the farms would be equivalent to about 200 billion barrels of oil. It would not, then, be cheap energy. But if the output were hydrogen,* and if it was sold at a price per heat-unit value corresponding to present oil prices, then the revenues could be sufficient to cover the amortization of the solar energy plants, which we are assuming have lifetimes of thirty to forty years. Once solar energy is, so to speak, mass produced, the costs of operating the farms should diminish, and their lifetime surely can be extended far beyond thirty or forty years.

The scientific feasibility of thermal conversion of solar energy has been proven, but as far as engineering implementation is concerned, we are still at the beginning. If governments are willing to fund research as generously as

---

* Solar energy farms will be situated far away from industrial centers, and therefore pipelines will have to join energy producer and user (as is the case with oil). It is probable that the plant will, through catalytic or electrolytic processes, convert solar radiation into a transportable substance such as hydrogen.

they funded nuclear energy, space exploration and supersonic aircraft, operational feasibility and economic reality should be achieved rather quickly. So far, unfortunately, no such funding is in sight. Perhaps it is because solar energy, unlike nuclear energy, has no military potential.

As we propose the implementation of a program which our world computer model suggests is feasible and desirable, we take certain things for granted. We assume that as coal is reexploited as a source of energy, old, destructive mining practices will give way to new procedures that will restore the environment, not leave it barren. We assume that coal gasification and liquefication plants will be built, and will be joined by efficient worldwide distribution systems. But mostly we assume—or at least hope—that our life-styles will change, that we, the consumers, will understand that our frivolous use of energy takes food from the mouths of children. We assume that no one who knows the situation will continue to call "economic growth" a system that gives us more and more material goods while peoples elsewhere starve. Those of us who live in the Developed World have, we are told, the highest standard of living the world has ever known. That assertion is made in reference to the material goods we possess. But if we knowingly consume less energy, if we deliberately own fewer goods, if we consciously simplify our lives just a little so that others may have only the minimal goods and food to be alive, then what, really, will happen to our standard of living? Won't the standard—the moral standard—really rise?

We are not the Developed World; we are actually the *over*developed world. Economic growth in a world where regions are underdeveloped is fundamentally contrary to mankind's social, moral, organizational, and scientific growth.

At this moment in history we are facing an enormously difficult decision. For the first time in man's life on earth, he is being asked to refrain from doing what he can do; he is being asked to restrain his economic and technological advancement, or at least to direct it differently from before; he is being asked by all the future generations of the earth to share his good fortune with the unfortunate—not in a spirit of charity, but in a spirit of necessity. He is being asked to concentrate now on the organic growth of the total world system. Can he, in good conscience, say no?

CHAPTER 11

Epilogue

The results of the computer analysis reported in this book provide answers to the basic questions posed in Chapter 2 on the conditions required for the solution of the major world crises and the strategies leading to that solution. In particular, we have seen that:

1. *The current crises are not temporary,* but rather reflect a persistent trend inherent in the historical pattern of development.
2. *The solution of these crises can be developed only in a global context* with full and explicit recognition of the emerging world system and on a long-term basis. This would necessitate, among others changes, a new world economic order and a global resources allocation system.
3. *The solutions cannot be achieved by traditional means* confined to an isolated aspect of the world system, such

as economics. What is really needed is nothing short of a complete integration of all strata in our hierarchical view of world development—that is, a simultaneous consideration of all aspects of mankind's evolution from individual values and attitudes to ecological and environmental conditions.

4. *It is possible to resolve these crises through cooperation rather than confrontation;* indeed, in most instances cooperation is equally beneficial to all participants. The greatest obstacles to cooperation are the short-term gains that might be obtained through confrontation. Even if these gains are short-lived and demonstrably lead to long-term losses, there is always a pressure to go after these gains.

In general, the strategies for solution of the crisis in world development demonstrate the necessity for organic growth of the world system. Indeed, that appears to be the only way to prevent major regional, if not global, catastrophes. Furthermore, it is a "natural" way to control the undifferentiated growth which is taking place in different ways in various parts of the world. In such a case there would be no need for special "no-growth" policies. On the other hand, failure to develop a master plan which will allow mankind to progress into organic development would make "surgical measures" to control cancerous growth inevitable.

What are the immediate first steps which could be taken on a social or individual basis and which can create an atmosphere in which serious attempts to develop master plans for organic growth can be undertaken? On the societal level the necessary changes include:

1. The realization that *counterproductivity* will be the ultimate consequence of any action confined solely to

short-term considerations. This must be accepted as a basic premise in all decision-making processes. Long-term assessment ought to become standard procedure in the consideration of fundamental decisions regarding developmental issues. Only in such a way can organizations—businesses, governments, or international units—actively contribute and consciously influence the emerging world system. Otherwise they might very well become nothing more than passive passengers on a voyage charted by outside forces.

2. *The futility of narrow nationalism* must be appreciated and taken as an axiom in the decision-making framework. *Global issues can be solved only by global concerted action.* For example, any nation that will try to solve the pervasive problem of inflation by actions limited solely to measures within its own boundary will be doomed to disappointment. Similarly, even if only a few countries resist such measures, the effort will almost certainly remain futile.

3. Development of a practical *international framework* in which the *cooperation* essential for the emergence of a new mankind on an organic growth path will become a *matter of necessity* rather than being left to good will and preference. Balance between constituent parts of the world system is needed to achieve that end; among other implications this suggests the need for stronger regional arrangements and accelerated development in certain parts of the world. Such developments are in the best interest of all regions, i.e., the entire globe.

4. Realization of the *overriding importance of the long-term global development crises,* as discussed in this report, and willingness to place this highest on the

agenda of the issues to be dealt with explicitly by national governments and international organizations. Precisely because the symptoms of these global crises might become fully visible only toward the end of the century, the time to act is now; when the symptoms become clear the remedy will no longer be possible, as has been shown repeatedly in this report. Future history will not focus on personality and social classes, as has been characteristic of history in the past, but on the use of resources and survival of the human species. The time to affect that history is *now*.

The last item requires certain elaboration: Governments and international organizations are currently too preoccupied with military alliances and bloc politics. But this problem is becoming of secondary importance, because a nuclear war could clearly result in a suicidal holocaust and can no longer be counted among rational alternatives. Therefore, barring suicide, mankind will face the most awesome test in its history: the necessity of a change in the man-nature relationship and the emergence of a new perception of mankind as a living global system. Failure to prepare for such a development will surely increase national and regional competition, leading eventually to ever more sharply focused military polarization, and to increased likelihood of tipping the balance toward a nuclear world war and thus mankind's suicide. Hence, *there is no more urgent task in the quest for peace than to help guide the world system onto the path of organic growth through the various stages of its evolution through cooperation rather than confrontation.* Finding a way to avoid major confrontations, which will surely come when any of the world-regions faces the prospect of collapse, is a far greater contribution to peace than the current haggling about boundaries and alliances.

Regarding individual values and attitudes the following lessons seem to be outstanding for the new global ethic implicit in the preceding requirements.

1. *A world consciousness* must be developed through which every individual realizes his role as a member of the world community. Famine in Tropical Africa should be considered as relevant and as disturbing to a citizen of Germany as famine in Bavaria. It must become part of the consciousness of every individual that "the basic unit of human cooperation and hence survival is moving from the national to the global level." *

2. A *new ethic in the use of material resources* must be developed which will result in a style of life compatible with the oncoming age of scarcity. This will require a new technology of production based on minimal use of resources and longevity of products rather than production processes based on maximal throughput. One should be proud of saving and conserving rather than of spending and discarding.

3. An *attitude toward nature must be developed based on harmony rather than conquest.* Only in this way can man apply in practice what is already accepted in theory—that is, that man is an integral part of nature.

4. If the human species is to survive, man must develop a *sense of identification with future generations* and be ready to trade benefits to the next generations for the benefits to himself. If each generation aims at maximum good for itself, *Homo Sapiens* is as good as doomed.

* Edwin Reischauer, *Toward the 21st Century: Education for a Changing World.* (New York: Alfred A. Knopf, 1973.)

The changes in social and individual attitudes which we are recommending require a new kind of education; an education geared to the twenty-first century rather than the twentieth or nineteenth centuries. It is not too early to inaugurate the necessary changes. "Children starting first grade today will hardly become real operating members of the society before the year 2000. The twenty-first century is not that far away when you think in terms of basic education." "The subject matter of education should be fundamentally mankind—the human experience." *

We have considered in some detail in this report the prospects for mankind's development over a fifty-year period. However, a look even beyond a fifty-year period is necessary to provide a feel for the trends underlying critical developments in human society. After all, difficult as it is to effect a change, it is even more difficult to undo one.

Once the time horizon is extended beyond fifty years, one has to begin to consider the "outer limits," † the limits that man cannot transgress without destroying himself and the biosphere.

One of the most fascinating outer limits, and at the same time one with the gravest possible consequences, concerns man's impact on climate. Two opposite trends are active in this respect: (1) a continuous increase in CO_2 content in the atmosphere which could result in a steady rise in temperature around the globe; (2) an increase in the suspended particulate matter in the atmosphere as a consequence of man's agricultural and industrial activities which could re-

---

* *Ibid.*

† A term coined by Maurice Strong, Executive Director of the United Nations Environmental Program.

sult in a temperature decline. Since 1945 the second trend has appeared to be prevailing. If it continues it will have grave consequences for food production capacity of the globe and therefore on the entire world system. On the other hand, an increase in waste heat associated with increased energy production will create heat islands which, coupled with increased CO_2 in the atmosphere, might lead to a progressive warming of the Northern Hemisphere.* This entails the possibility of an irreversible melting of the Arctic Sea ice with tremendous climatological consequences —a slow process to be sure, but one which can be speeded up considerably by the actions of man in pursuit of short-term gains (see Brief on Oil Spills and Ice Melting).

Brief on Oil Spills and Ice Melting

A particular danger lies in the all too real possibility of large oil spills during the exploitation of the oil reserves in the Arctic Ocean. This might lead to melting of the Arctic Sea ice when emulsified oil droplets are distributed by ocean currents and then accumulate on the underside of the sea ice. Since the ice melts on top and freezes on the bottom, the accumulated oil will gradually move upward and the surface of the sea ice will ultimately darken, thus reducing its reflectivity (albedo). This will drastically increase the heat absorption of the ice during periods of strong sunshine (insolation), starting an irreversible melting process. After the ice has melted the albedo of the now open ocean is so reduced compared with the former white sea ice cover that the water's increased heat absorption will prevent its refreezing. After the complete melting of the sea ice, the constant addition of "sweet" melted ice water to the ocean is stopped so that the present thick upper layer of sea water with low salt content is gradually replaced by water

* T. Bergeron, Monograph *Amer. Geophs. Union* 5 (1960), 399.

of higher salinity whose freezing temperature is lower, thus making the refreezing of the Arctic Ocean even less likely. An open Arctic Ocean would cause a shift of all climatic zones by several hundred miles. Such regions as the Mediterranean, California, the Punjab, and others would predominantly become constantly arid savannahs, with disastrous implications for agriculture.

Another "outer limit" may be reached by the rapid increase of water consumption, particularly because of the fast growing area of irrigated land. The amount of water evaporation * over irrigated soil already amounts to 1700 cubic kilometers, or more than 400 cubic miles per year. This staggering figure corresponds to 350 gallons per day for every person living today. The growth of the world's population will force bringing under the plough more and more arable soil in the arid and semiarid regions. Eventually,† the water for irrigation ‡ would soar to more than twenty times the present consumption—to nearly 10,000 cubic miles per year. (See Brief on Irrigation.)

Brief on Irrigation

Securing the irrigation water necessary to meet growing demand for food production over the next fifty years would pose, among others, the following two problems.
1. Such huge amounts of water cannot be taken from the runoff and the ground water in the arid and semi-arid zones. At least half must be obtained through desalination of sea water. Even if it were possible to reduce greatly the energy requirements for desalination (from today's 15–20 kilowatt

---

* H. Flohn, "Der Wasserhauchalt der Erde," in *Naturwissenschaften* 60 (1973), 310–348.

† Monograph *Amer. Geophys. Union* 5 (1960), 399.

‡ A water layer seven to nine feet thick is needed yearly for the irrigation of arid land.

hours per cubic meter), five to ten times the present total global energy consumption would be needed to desalinate the sea water required for irrigation. To gain a better impression of this vast amount of energy, suppose every person on earth today consumed as much energy as the average American citizen: the total energy thus consumed would be equivalent to the energy then used just for desalination purposes.

2. *The evaporation of the irrigation water would in such a case amount to about 30 percent of the current rate of natural evaporation over land. Thus the hydrological cycle over land would be greatly accelerated with as yet unknown climatological consequences.*

Other climatological changes loom if nuclear fast-breeder power reactors were to be utilized. The enormous concentration of power production in nuclear parks would involve not only the disposal of vast amounts of waste heat into the water, but would constitute as well huge "heat islands," where the artificially generated energy would by far surpass the heat input of solar radiation. Our ignorance concerning the effects of such practices should not lead us to overlook the danger that strong local disturbances can produce small shifts in the general circulation of the atmosphere which, on the global scale, might result in considerable changes in weather and climate for larger regions.

But there are still other limits, "inner" rather than "outer," the limits within man himself. They are no less real because it is man who is ultimately the generator of change and the watchdog who keeps it from getting out of control. As Aurelio Peccei has stressed: "We generally neglect these limits because they are imponderable, and concern the noosphere, the field of the intellect, of reason, of understanding oneself and the world, and finally of the spirit. Man has committed himself so deeply to constructing ever larger and more complex artificial systems that it has become difficult for him to control them, thereby losing a sense of his destiny and at the same time that of his communion with Nature and with the transcendent. No one can say with certainty; but psychic and social damage, evident above all in the great conurbations, warn us that inner limits have perhaps been surpassed, that our minds and our nervous systems cannot take much more overloading." *

Nor are the organizational limits to be forgotten. Complexity in an organization increases at a faster rate than its size. The increase in human population and sophistication of technology and modern living increases tremendously the size, and therefore even more, the complexity of the organizations essential to support what we have come to believe to be a civilized life. Moreover, the efficiency of the organization decreases rapidly with the complexity, since additional overhead and infrastructure are needed just to "keep things going." The developed world is experiencing an appreciable decline in quality and quantity of services in spite of an almost unbearable increase in cost; from medical to transportation and postal services, one can find an abundance of examples to prove the point. Serious attention should be given to how our societies could cope with the global crises and "inner limits" problem. No wonder that alienation within society is becoming more widespread, and that more people resort to desperate action in a vain search for change.

If the limits are discernible, a strategy is needed to avert catastrophic encounters with such limits. These encounters would be a new phenomenon in the history of mankind,

* "The Real Limits to Growth," personal communication to The Club of Rome, 1973.

which requires a new strategy to deal with the very question of survival. *Underlying these "limits-crises" is a gap be-between man and nature which is widening at an alarming rate. To bridge that gap man has to develop a new attitude to nature based on harmonious relationship rather than conquest.* When the problem of narrowing that gap becomes truly apparent and obviously inescapable, many issues which appear very pressing and urgent in the present socio-political arena might well be resolved by the very fact that the options would be reduced so much that hardly any would be left.* So fundamental a reorientation cannot take place, however, unless there is a sense of community, of a common destiny. And this requires, inevitably, that the second gap—between "North" and "South," rich and poor—be bridged. One part of humanity cannot undergo such a fundamental change while the rest flounders. Even if such a course were attempted, it would be of little use since the dilemma is truly global. Mankind, confronted by an unbridged and ever widening gap, simply cannot face the *problématique humaine* with any hope of success. Closing that gap is therefore a matter of universal common concern.

What is to be done meanwhile? First, an essential prerequisite is understanding the nature of the gap between regions. It is not only a question of economics, of transferring investment funds, even though that is the very first and inevitable step. Many thoughtful observers have stated repeatedly that the developing part of the world should not and will not follow the path traversed by the more developed world. Yet, with the transfer of investment capital

* Arnold Toynbee, *Observer* (London), 1974.

goes the transfer of technology, and with the transfer of technology goes the transfer of ways and means of doing things. High-sounding statements notwithstanding, a new path has yet to be found. And it might very well become imperative if the gap is to be closed in any real sense.

Second, since the change is to be brought about by men, there must exist a framework conducive to development in the desired direction. As already pointed out above, our analyses of the world system have indicated quite clearly that the "most preferable solutions" always involve "harmony" or "compromise" among "balanced" participants. But there is no balance between participants like the United States or the Soviet Union on one hand and Dahomey or Singapore on the other. In order to achieve *balance between regions in global development a more coherent regional outlook must be developed in various parts of the world* so that the "preferable solutions" will be arrived at of necessity rather than out of good will, a quality not common even among those who can "afford" it. We are not talking of any regional regimentation. Indeed, such a trend would be in contradiction to the need for change and most probably would make it impossible. Rather, we are talking about a regional sense of common destiny that will find its expression through appropriate societal, economic, and political arrangements and the formulation of regional economic concepts and objectives. Just like the "new path for development," these new arrangements are yet to be explicated and will most probably emerge through the very process of development. But they are surely essential, as our entire analysis of the world system indicates. Such a regional outlook will create a "critical mass" necessary for the practical implementation of new and innovative ways of functioning in cultural, economic, and agricultural areas, especially on the rural level.* Instead of trying to "outperform" the developed world by traversing the same path in a much shorter time, various regions should develop their own ways and means, as well as methods, to absorb most effectively whatever is transferred from the developed world in money or in kind.

It should also be clear that we are not talking about "globalism" in the sense that favors uniformity—that is, in the sense of a monolithic world system: one language, one structure, one government, etc. As in natural ecological systems, diversity is the key for adaptation, which in turn is the key to survival. Again, by analogy with nature, however, diversity must exist in harmony if it is to contribute to adaptation of the system as a whole. Diversity of tradition and culture, a feeling for one's own place under the sun, is essential in order to mobilize the moral strength surely necessary for the required magnitude of change.

Third, global anticipatory and adjustment procedures and mechanisms must be developed to deal with a stream of crises, which might well come in increasingly short succession, as the results of our study indicate. Crises now must be prevented rather than reacted to. Today they gain great momentum and reach terrifying proportions in far less time than is needed for the design, operationalization, and implementation of political, social, and technological remedies. Measures prompted by a crisis at our doorsteps will be effective only ten to twenty years from now, when the qualitative and quantitative aspects of the crisis will most

---

* M. Guernier, "Les communautes villageoises," personal note to The Club of Rome, 1974.

likely appear in completely different form than at present.
A region's present energy crisis might then have grown into
catastrophic food shortages in quite different parts of the
world, or into general economic deterioration and social up-
heavals.

Hence, there is an urgent need for an "instrument" that
can be used to test alternative plans for anticipatory action;
to evaluate the realizability of these plans in the face of
national, regional, and global constraints; to determine
whether short-term benefits in one area might not entail
great harm in others or even destroy future long-term options. Such a planning instrument must be representable in
credible, yet understandable terms, not only to decision-
makers and the "elite," but to the public at large. For there
should be no misunderstandings: Some short-term losses
would most certainly have to be accepted for the sake of
long-term gains; some sacrifices will be required from everybody for the sake of later generations and orderly world
development, and the political decision-makers as well as
the public will have to be persuaded to abandon their usual
practice based on the belief that "a problem postponed
is . . . half solved." This can result only from a careful
assessment of alternatives which in turn cannot be conceived
without a credible comprehensive planning instrument en-
abling the national leaders to find solutions to the over-
riding problems in the global context. The multilevel world
model on which this report is based is a first step in that
direction.

Mankind cannot afford to wait for change to occur spon-
taneously and fortuitously. Rather, man must initiate on his
own changes of necessary but tolerable magnitude in time to
avert intolerably massive and externally generated change.

A strategy for such change can be evolved only in the spirit of truly global cooperation, shaped in free partnership by the world's diverse regional communities and guided by a rational master plan for long-term organic growth. All our computer simulations have shown quite clearly that this is the only sensible and feasible approach to avoid major regional and ultimately global catastrophe,.and that the time that can be wasted before developing such a global world system is running out. *Clearly the only alternatives are division and conflict, hate and destruction.*

Collaborators and Consultants

B = Braunschweig
C = Cleveland
He = Heidelberg
H = Hannover
K = Karlsruhe
N = Nymwegen
G = Grenoble

The following lists contain the names of scientists actively involved in the construction of the regionalized multilevel world model which is used for the analysis as described in this report, or providing consultation on specific issues regarding the model. The responsibility for the analysis itself, as described in this report and its interpretation, is solely that of the authors.

Directors

Prof. Dr. Mihajlo Mesarovic, Cleveland, USA
Prof. Dr.-Ing. Dr. h.c. Eduard Pestel, Hannover, Germany

Collaborators

He   Dipl. agr. H.J. Baessler; food, agricultural ecology
H   Mr. R. Bauerschmidt; energy resources
C   Mrs. Shelly Baum; technical preparation

H	Dipl.-Ing. H. Billib; water resources
K	Dr. H. Bossel; systems analysis, energy
C	Mr. C. Brewer; political science
C	Mrs. M. L. Cantini; technical preparation
C	Mr. N. Chu; systems analysis
C	Dr. W. Clapham; food and ecology
H	Dr. R. Denton; energy
C	Dr. A. Erdilek; economics
H	Dipl.-Ing. P. Gille; computer coordination, programming, software
H	Dipl.-Ing. H. Gottwald; environmental impacts
C	Mr. J. Huerta; water resources
C	Dr. B. Hughes; political science; energy
C	Mrs. J. Kirk; population
N	Dr. J. Klabbers; water resources
H	Dr. W. Kleeberg; water resources
H	Mr. H. Kreczik; illustrations
C	Mr. K. Kominek; systems analysis and simulation
C	Dr. A. Kuper; energy
C	Mr. C. Loxley; economics
H	Dipl.-Ing. H. J. Maier; energy
C	Mr. N. Matsuda; population
C	Dr. M. McCarthy; economics
C	Mr. A. Mesarovic; data processing
C	Mr. J. Morris; data processing
H	Dr. P. Oehmen; population
B	Dr. W. Paul; population
H	Dr. R. Pestel; scientific coordination, economics, ecology
G	Dr. F. Rechenmann; computer science
C	Dr. J. Richardson; political science
H	Dr. W. Richter; agriculture
C	Miss M. Schaefer; technical preparation

C Mr. T. Shook; computer and systems analysis
H Dipl. Math & rer. pol. W. Stroebele; economics
H Dipl. rer. pol. M. Szabados; economics
C Dr. M. Teraguchi; ecology
C Mr. M. Warshaw; computer science
H Dr. P. Wiesenthal; computer science
C Mr. R. Young; geology
C Miss J. Ziffer; data processing

Consultants

Prof. Dr.-Ing. Dr.h.c. H. Billib; Hannover, water resources
Dr. M. Cardenas; Mexico City; water resources
Prof. Dr. U. Colombo, Milan; resources
Prof. Dr. W. Egger, Heidelberg; environment
Prof. Dr. H. Ellenberg, Göttingen; general ecology
Prof. Dr. H. Flohn, Bonn; water resources, climate
Prof. Dr. B. Fritsch, Zurich; economics
Prof. Dr. D. Gabor, London; general studies, energy
Dr. M. Guernier, Paris; agriculture in developing countries
Prof. Dr. B. Hickman, Stanford; economics
Dr. W. Hohn, Hannover; resources
Prof. Dr. J. Hrones, Cleveland; systems
Prof. Dr. H. Hubel, Hannover; economics
Mr. D. Jacobs; editorial assistance
Prof. Dr. L. Klein, Philadelphia; economics
Prof. Dr. J. Mermet, Grenoble; computer science
Dr. h.c. G. Sassmannshausen, Hannover; resources
Prof. Dr. P. Schachtschebel, Hannover; agriculture
Prof. Dr. Y. Takahara, Tokyo; multilevel systems
Prof. Dr. F. Ullrich, Göttingen; agriculture ecology
Prof. Dr. J. Wehrmann, Hannover; agriculture

Countries as Grouped in Regions 1-10

Region 1. North America

Canada   United States of America

Region 2. Western Europe

Andorra	Italy
Austria	Liechtenstein
Belgium	Luxembourg
Denmark	Malta
Federal Republic of Germany	Monaco
Finland	Netherlands
France	Norway
Great Britain	Portugal
Greece	San Marino
Iceland	Spain
Ireland	Sweden

Switzerland   Yugoslavia
Turkey

Region 3. Japan

Region 4. Rest of the Developed Market Economies

Australia   Oceania
Israel   South Africa
New Zealand   Tasmania

Region 5. Eastern Europe

Albania   Hungary
Bulgaria   Poland
Czechoslovakia   Rumania
German Democratic Republic   Soviet Union

Region 6. Latin America

Argentina   Guyana
Barbados   Haiti
Bolivia   Honduras
Brazil   Jamaica
British Honduras   Mexico
Chile   Nicaragua
Colombia   Panama
Costa Rica   Paraguay
Cuba   Peru
Dominican Republic   Surinam
Ecuador   Trinidad and Tobago
El Salvador   Uruguay
French Guiana   Venezuela
Guatemala

Region 7. North Africa and the Middle East

Abu Dhabi
Aden
Algeria
Bahrain
Cyprus
Dubai
Egypt
Iran
Iraq
Jordan
Kuwait

Lebanon
Libya
Masqat-Oman
Morocco
Qatar
Saudi Arabia
Syria
Trucial Oman
Tunisia
Yemen

Region 8. Main Africa

Angola
Burundi
Cabinda
Cameroon
Central African Republic
Chad
Dahomey
Ethiopia
French Somali Coast
Gabon
Gambia
Ghana
Guinea
Ivory Coast
Kenya
Liberia
Malagasy Republic
Malawi

Mali
Mauritania
Mauritius
Mozambique
Niger
Nigeria
Portuguese Guinea
Republic of Congo
Reunion
Rhodesia
Rwanda
Senegal
Sierra Leone
Somalia
South Africa
South West Africa
Spanish Guinea
Spanish Sahara

Sudan   Upper Volta
Tanzania   Zaire
Togo   Zambia
Uganda

Region 9. South and Southeast Asia

Afghanistan   Malaysia
Bangladesh   Nepal
Burma   Pakistan
Cambodia   Philippines
Ceylon   South Korea
India   South Vietnam
Indonesia   Taiwan
Laos   Thailand

Region 10. Centrally Planned Asia

Mongolia   North Vietnam
North Korea   People's Republic of China

Additional Briefs

(A) BRIEF ON SOME FACTS ON THE EXPANSION OF FOOD PRODUCTION

With rapidly declining world food stocks that amount today to only a thirty-day reserve, humanity is literally living from hand to mouth. If the cycle of prolonged dry weather periods in the United States—like the Dust Bowl days of the 1930s—were to recur, poor harvest periods might lie around the corner even for North America, the producer of more than two thirds of the world's exports in cereals and 90 percent of the exportable soybeans. The world has thus begun to depend to a dangerous degree on the outcome of the annual harvest in North America, and the hungry majority of the world lives under a veritable sword of Damocles that will drop and kill millions whenever that harvest fails. What is in store for the world in twenty to twenty-five years, when in South Asia alone there will be at least a billion more

mouths to feed; or fifteen years beyond that time when yet
another billion will most probably be added to the population in the same region?

With regard to the world food supply situation we are also
confronted by the fact that scarcity is produced not only by
the fast-rising number of hungry people, but also, and not
least, by the increasing demands of a growing affluent minority. Affluence is hunger's main competitor for the available
food supply. Although a human can certainly take only a
given amount of food in terms of quantity, the consumption
of food depends on the composition of the diet. Increased
affluence in various regions of the world, and even of certain
social strata within nations with a chronic deficit in food,
leads to the consumption of more meat, eggs, milk, etc., and
thus worsens the problem of food supply (see Table III
A–1); for, it takes, for example, an average of seven pounds
of grain to produce one pound of meat. To overcome this

TABLE III A–1: ANNUAL PRODUCTION OF MEAT PER INHABITANT

	1961–65	1970–71
North America	72 kg	82 kg
Western Europe	41	48
USSR	30	36
Latin America	32	30
Asia– { Near East	10	10
Far East	3	3
Africa	10	10

(Source: Institut d'études démographiques, Paris–d'après FAO)

grave consequence of affluence, it would be necessary to change rather drastically the life-styles and the pattern of food consumption in the industrialized nations. We would have to give up presently prevailing eating habits that, applied universally, would allow feeding with present agricultural output of only 1.2 billion people, not the nearly 4 billion living today.

Of course, food production will expand. There are four ways in which an appreciable increase in food production is possible:

1. Increase of the cultivated land area.
2. Increase of yield per unit of land through such technological inputs as fertilizer, high-yield seeds, irrigation, soil conservation measures, pesticides, herbicides, storage and transportaton facilities, mechanical equipment for tilling and harvesting, etc.
3. Increase of marine animal production.
4. Development of synthetic foods.

Regarding the first possibility, we refer to the Table III A–2.

We observe that the 1.5 billion hectares in the cultivation cycle, that is, having recently been cultivated—represent about 11 percent of the world's total land area of 13.5 billion hectares (52 million square miles), but 8 billion hectares, or 59 percent, of the world's total land area is deserts, salted, and ice-covered land or mountains. Much of the remainder is not suitable for cultivation. Thus, the figures in the table give us only a superficial picture of the possible increases of cultivated land in the ten world regions. There are still reserves in North America and to a lesser degree in Australia. The tables suggest that significant increases are also possible in Latin America and Main Africa.

TABLE III A–2: AGRICULTURAL LAND RESERVES

All land figures are in thousands
of hectares

Region	Ultimate Maximum Arable Land	Land in the Cultivation Cycle	Land Harvested per Year
1. North America	392,000	220,000	111,000
2. Western Europe	155,000	127,000	89,000
3. Japan	8,000	6,000	6,000
4. Australia, etc.	150,000	58,000	19,000
5. Eastern Europe (including USSR)	382,000	280,000	193,000
6. Latin America	429,000	128,000	77,000
7. North Africa and the Middle East	86,000	53,000	29,000
8. Main Africa	423,000	167,000	73,000
9. South Asia	278,000	268,000	235,000
10. China	122,000	118,000	100,000
World	2,425,000	1,425,000	932,000

But potentially arable land in these tropical areas is much
more difficult to find than in the temperate zones. The main
possible reserves are the vast uncultivated land areas now
covered by tropical rain forests in the Amazon Basin in
Brazil and in the Congo region of Main Africa. But once
the lush forests are cleared, the soils of these regions are
exceedingly vulnerable to the incessant rain and soon lose
their fertility. In some cases the soil even hardens irreversibly
to the texture of concrete, so that it is more suitable as a
building material than as an agricultural resource (Cambodia's Angkor Wat is built of this material, called laterite).
Few crops have been grown satisfactorily on a commercial

basis in the humid tropics, and these tend to be low-protein or non-food cash crops such as palm oil, sugar cane, bananas, coffee, cocoa, and latex. Even the native crops tend to be low-protein varieties such as cassava, yams, and plantains. Here the invention of a completely new agriculture will be necessary, either to develop tree-like plants that yield ordinary nourishing foods and can withstand the hot and humid climate or to generate a series of plants that grow under the cover of tropical trees, which protect them and their soil against the pounding of the heavy tropical rains that otherwise cause destruction by horizontal erosion or vertical washouts. For decades to come only minimal contributions to the solution of the world's food problem can be expected from the humid tropical zones. Not much more encouraging is the situation in the semiarid regions, the savannahs, ordinarily subjected to oscillations of rainy and dry seasons. Because of the uncertainties of the climate these zones are permanently under the menace of famines, as the recent past has shown only too tragically in the Sahel zone of Africa. Still, a proper coordination of all the research efforts presently carried on for the agricultural problems of these semiarid regions should be able to lead eventually to beneficial results, if only to stop, in the first instance, the southward advance of the desert in the African Sahel that has persisted for the past twenty years and by now has assumed an average annual rate of more than six miles.

Since the chances for a large expansion of the cultivated land area are quite limited, the hopes for increased food production rest chiefly on the belief that the presently cultivated land area could yield far greater amounts of food by manifold technological inputs in most parts of the developing countries (see also Table III A–3). This approach also forms the basis for the Provisional Indicative World Plan for Agricultural Development of the United Nations Food and Agriculture Organization (FAO) in Rome, 1970. However, the following arguments of the FAO report should serve to caution against much of the wishful thinking regarding greatly increased food production in the most critical developing regions of Tropical Africa and South Asia: ". . . climate, lack of assured water supply, poor soil fertility, and difficult topography, . . . and even where there are no over-riding physical obstacles, bad communications, long distances from markets, high costs of inputs, lack of credits, . . . and in many developing countries, land tenure systems . . . are serious obstacles to progress. . . ." Many others could be added, such as illiteracy, lack of proper infrastructure, etc. As to the "miracle" new seed varieties (Green Revolution) the report states: "Far from being miracles . . . they are still at an evolutionary stage and therefore far from perfect. This particularly applies to rice

TABLE III A–3: YIELDS—TOTAL CEREALS 1972

1. North America	3,452 kg/ha
2. Western Europe	3,150
3. Japan (two harvests per year)	5,497
4. Rest of Developed Market Economies	1,200
5. Eastern Europe	1,677
6. Latin America	1,439
7. North Africa and the Middle East	1,291
8. Main Africa	804
9. South and Southeast Asia	1,337
10. Centrally Planned Asia	1,794

(Source: FAO 1972)

in Asia, for which a number of serious pest and disease problems remain unsolved, and where the eating quality of the new varieties is also inferior to many traditional ones; and to millet and sorghum in Africa, where varieties, introduced from other continents, have so far had little success; while little work has been done on barley in most developing countries." Thus, long years of research and development are still ahead, while their success with regard to sustained high yield is far from assured. However, even if the increase in food were possible, it will most certainly depend on technological inputs of truly stunning dimensions which will be too expensive for the poverty-ridden countries, and fraught with grave ecological and social disruptions.

Further expansion of food production also leads to increasing pressure on the food-producing ecosystems. Wherever man settled he soon began to cut the forests down to gain land he could cultivate. As long as this was limited to comparatively small areas, the ecosystem remained intact. Now, however, in his urgent quest for food, man has again hastened the process of deforestation, most recklessly in some regions of the world, the Amazon and Congo Basin, for example, and even more the Indian subcontinent, all of which are threatened by progressive deforestation. In the Amazon and Congo Basins, the disastrous consequences of deforestation are instantly visible, so there is a good chance for the lesson to be learned quickly that this folly cannot be perpetuated without causing irreparable damage. But the damage that deforestation in Nepal, for example, does to agriculture in the plains of Pakistan, India, and Bangladesh is not directly seen by those who cut down the woods in Himalayan foothills, where all the major river systems of the Indian subcontinent originate. But even today the consequences of deforestation are only too apparent: no year passes without most severe floods that destroy land and harvest for many millions of people. But since most people think in short time horizons, deforestation continues and the already insufficient food-producing capacity of large parts of South Asia will surely be further undermined by future larger flood catastrophes.

Another similar and no less tragic result of fast-growing human and livestock population pressure on food-producing ecosystems is visible in the four-thousand-mile-long fringe stretching south of the Sahara from Senegal all the way across Africa to Ethiopia. Denuding the semiarid landscape by deforestation and overgrazing has enabled the desert to move southward, in some cases up to thirty miles a year, particularly in the years plagued by increasing droughts. Also this has become a long-term problem because of the insupportable pressure on this already delicate ecosystem; it is decidedly not a temporary catastrophe caused by prolonged dry periods that could be taken care of by rushing several hundred thousand tons of grain into the area as soon as television camera teams have brought the agony of men, women, children, and animals into our well-fed homes.

There are also less dramatic consequences of man's pressure on the food-producing ecosystems that come with excessive use of fertilizer and chemical pesticides and herbicides. These not only affect the microorganisms in the producing soil; they also eutrophicate rivers, ponds, and lakes and thereby drastically reduce their oxygen-producing capacity, and they wander along the food chain in ever greater concentrations so that finally they became harmful even to man. Finally, there is the pressure on the climate that a vastly increased area of irrigated land would exert (see Chapter 11), and the ecologically destablizing effect of the big dams and irrigation projects. For example, the Aswan Dam of Egypt has been instrumental in an epidemic of schistosomiasis among the peasants farming in the Nile valley; it has caused a deterioration in the fertility of the soil by retaining the Nile's famous alluvial silt, and it has caused a significant reduction of fish in the Eastern Mediterranean six hundred miles away by reducing the amount of fresh water entering the sea.

Marine fish currently provide 15 percent of the world's animal protein supplies. But the ecosystem producing fish is also seriously threatened by man's ruthless employment of ancient and modern fishing technologies. On the coasts of Europe and Asia dragnets have been scraping the ocean floor and thereby destroying for many years the beds of algae where the fish feed and lay their eggs. And off the Peruvian coast the modern fish-pumping techniques, which produced in the years 1969 to 1971 a bumper crop of anchovies, caused the Anchoveta to vanish and hardly anyone still believes that this disappearance is just temporary. Formerly optimistic experts are now convinced that it will be some years before the Anchoveta fishery, which accounted for 20 percent of the world's fish cash, might recover.

In ten years food-needy man's back will be even closer to the wall, and in another ten years still closer. Is there really a chance that he will relax his pressure on the ecosystem, or will he continue all over the world to inflict irreparable damage on nature, which then will retaliate inexorably and mercilessly?

(B) BRIEF ON FOSSIL FUEL RESERVES

On January 1, 1973, the proven resources of oil amounted to nearly 90 billion tons, or 667 billion barrels (1 metric ton of crude oil = 7.47 barrels), which at the 1972 consumption level, about 2.5 billion tons, would last thirty-seven years. But with a global consumption growth rate of 5 percent the reserves would have a lifetime of only twenty-one years (see Table III B–1). New oil discoveries are made

TABLE III B–1: REGIONAL TABLE OF OIL RESERVES

Oil reserves (in thousands of barrels) [2]

| | | | | Life-Indices | |
Region	Proven Reserves [1]		Production (1972)	Static	Dynamic 5% [3]
1	*2*	*3*	*4*	*5*	*6*
1. North America	47,023,271	7.1%	4,011,350	12	9
2. Western Europe	12,632,000	1.9%	157,680	80	33
3. Japan	23,000	0.003%	5,475	4	4
4. Australia, etc.	2,354,460	0.3%	157,206	15	11
5. Eastern Europe	78,500,000	11.8%	3,066,000	26	17
6. Latin America	32,601,750	4.9%	1,739,079	19	14
7. Middle East	438,894,000	65.8%	7,519,110	58	28
8. Main Africa	22,801,000	3.4%	754,638	30	19
9. South Asia	12,553,800	1.9%	543,084	23	16
10. China	19,500,000	2.9%	186,150	105	38
World	666,883,281	100%	18,140,122	37	21

[1] The data on proven reserves were reported by the *Oil and Gas Journal* (December 25, 1972); annual oil production was taken from the same source.
[2] 1 metric ton of oil = 7.47 barrels.
[3] Growth rate.

TABLE III B–2: REGIONAL TABLE OF GAS RESERVES [1]

Gas reserves (10⁹ m³) [5, 8]

$$\text{Gas reserves } (10^9 \ m^3)$$ [5, 8]

				Life-Indices	
				Static	Dy-namic 5%
Region	Proven Reserves		Production (1972) [2]		
1	2	3	4	5	6
1. North America	9,244	17.3%	713	13	10
2. Western Europe	5,056	9.5%	124	41	22
3. Japan	11	0.02%	3	4	4
4. Australia, etc.	1,509	2.8%	3	438	64
5. Eastern Europe	18,219	34.2%	264	69	31
6. Latin America	2,243	4.2%	93	24	16
7. Middle East	13,733	25.8%	55	248	53
8. Main Africa	1,359	2.5%	2	648	72
9. South Asia	1,348	2.5%	13	101	37
10. China	595	1.1%	4	150	44
World	53,317 [3, 7]	100% [6]	1,299 [4]	41	23

[1] Data on proven reserves were reported by the *Oil and Gas Journal* (December 25, 1972).

[2] Production numbers are taken from Felix, Fremont, *The Future of Energy Supply: "The Long Haul,"* 1973.

[3] Estimates reported by Felix, Fremont, *The Future of Energy Supply: "The Long Haul"* totals to 53,719 × 10⁹ m³.

[4] When added, total of column 6 may not equal the world total as some individual figures are not available.

[5] Conversion factor used: 1 m³ = 35.3149 cu.ft.

[6] When added, total column 3 may not equal 100% on account of round-off errors in individual numbers.

[7] 750 m³ natural gas is equivalent to 1 metric ton of coal.

[8] The presently highest estimate of recoverable gas reserve is eight times the proven reserves.

TABLE III B–3: REGIONAL TABLE OF COAL RESERVES

Total Coal (in millions of metric ton of coal equivalent) [1]

Region	Identified Reserves		Produc-tion [2]	Static	Dynamic 2% [3]
				Life-Indices	
1	2	3	4	5	6
1. North America	688,025	16.5%	556	1,237	164
2. Western Europe	70,673	1.7%	385	184	78
3. Japan	10,057	0.24%	40	253	91
4. Australia, etc.	68,652	1.65%	110	652	131
5. Eastern Europe	2,457,348	59.13%	821	2,993	207
6. Latin America	11,097	0.27%	9	1,214	163
7. Middle East	58	0.001%	1	75	46
8. Main Africa	6,588	0.16%	4	1,555	175
9. South Asia	56,855	1.32%	88	646	133
10. China	786,303	18.92%	396	1,988	187
World	4,155,656	100%	2,410	1,725	180

Most of the data were taken from Proceedings of the World Power Conference 1968, with the exception of the data on China (*Die Energiewirtschaft der Volksrepublik China,* Verlag Glueckauf 1973). With the new interest in coal, there might soon be higher figures available, due to intensified exploration and corresponding discoveries of new deposits. However, even a doubling of the total reserves would, for a constant growth rate of 2%, increase the life time of the resources only by 35 years, i.e., from 180 to 215 years.

[1] The figures shown are the summation of Anthracite, Bituminous and Sub-Bituminous coal—amounting to 80% of the total tonnage—and of Lignite and Brown Coal: which average half the calorific power. A weighted average of 25 Quadrillion BTU per Metric Ton is suggested as the energy equivalent of the combined total.

[2] Coal production data (1970) are taken from: *World Energy Supplies, 1961–70,* UN Series J. No. 15.

[3] Growth rate.

all the time but the rate is definitely decreasing while costs increase tremendously. The capital cost and the technical unit cost for oil from the North Sea, for example, are at least ten times greater than those in the Persian Gulf. For newly discovered offshore oil, and particularly for deep-sea reservoirs, even higher costs must be expected, not counting the possibly extreme "external costs" resulting from the creation of unforeseen environmental risks. Furthermore, to preserve a moderately comfortable future ratio between proven reserves and current annual production of crude oil, new oil deposits of the Alaskan North Slopes' or the North Sea's magnitude would soon be necessary every year, should oil consumption continue at predicted growth rates. It must be remembered that at an annual growth rate of 5 percent even doubled reserves would be exhausted after just another fourteen years. Taking the most optimistic estimates of recoverable oil reserves (including oil shale and tar sands) as being about 500 billion tons (about six times the presently proven resources), continued increases in oil consumption would deplete the reserves around 2030, little more than fifty years from now.

The natural gas situation is very similar (see Table III B–2). On the other hand the reserves of coal are far greater, having a static life index of nearly 2000 years (see Table III B–3).

(C) BRIEF ON OIL PRODUCTION COST, TRADE, AND CONSUMPTION

The outstanding feature of the present oil situation has to be viewed in terms of the fact that nearly two thirds of the proven reserves are in the areas of the Persian Gulf and

North Africa, where the capital cost of a barrel per day and the technical cost per barrel at the wellhead (transportation, government's revenues, and producing company's profit not included) are extremely low (see Table III C–1).*

TABLE III C–1

Energy Source	Cost in U.S. Dollars Capital Cost	Technical Unit Cost
Persian Gulf	100–300	0.10–0.20
Nigeria	600–800	0.40–0.60
Venezuela	700–1000	0.40–0.60
North Sea	2500–4000	0.90–2.00
Large deep-sea reservoirs	over 3000?	2.00–?
New U.S. reservoirs (not too remote)	3000–4000	2.00–2.50
Easy part of Alberta tar sands	3000–5000	2.00–3.00
High-grade oil shales	3000–7000	3.00–4.50
Gas synthesized from coal	5000–8000	3.00–6.00
Liquid synthesized from coal	6000–8000	3.00–6.00
Liquid natural gas (landed)	6000–9000	3.00–6.00

The holders of such huge reserves at low technical cost possess a virtual monopoly on cheap oil that gives them the freedom to raise the price of crude oil to what, in their opinion, the oil market is prepared to pay, as well as to impose production ceilings. The era of cheap oil has ended more quickly than expected and in a manner beyond the worst fears of the "best-informed" oil economists, because of the virtual monopoly of the OPEAC-countries on oil of very low technical unit cost.

* A. B. Looius, "Energy Resources," paper at the UN symposium on population, resources, and environment, Stockholm, 1973.

Figure IIIC-1

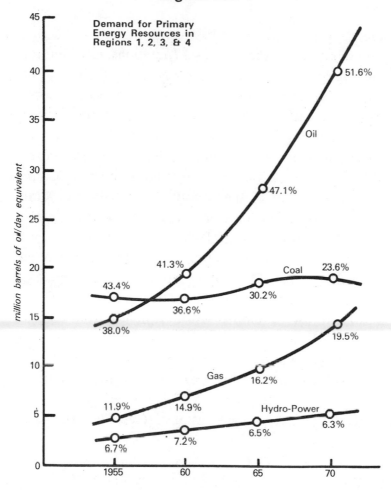

Demand for Primary
Energy Resources in
Regions 1, 2, 3, & 4

million barrels of oil/day equivalent

Oil 51.6%

47.1%

41.3%

43.4%

Coal 23.6%

36.6% 30.2%

38.0%

Gas 19.5%

16.2%

11.9% 14.9%

Hydro-Power

6.5% 6.3%

6.7% 7.2%

1955   60   65   70

Figure IIIC-2
Comparison of Primary Energy Components as Used in 1970

	Hydro-Power	Gas	Coal	Oil
Regions 1 2 3 & 4	6.3%	18.5%	23.6%	51.6%
Regions 5 & 10	3.1%	15.5%	59.0%	22.4%

There are great differences between production and consumption of energy in the world's 173 nations. Of the total, 110 must import two thirds and more of their supply; seventeen must import one to two thirds of their energy needs. Hence, nearly one third of the world's total primary energy—90 percent of its crude oil—moves through a vast global trade network. Of this oil, 90 percent is supplied by the OPEC (Organization of Petroleum Exporting Countries); more than half of the supply comes from the Arab nations (OPEAC). On the other hand, 80 percent of the traded oil 1.5 billion tons in 1970, or 10 billion barrels) goes to the industrialized nations, including the United States, Canada, Japan, Australia, and Western Europe.

The graph on the next page shows clearly how the "Western" nations of the developed world switched from coal to oil when, after World War II, the "cheap" Arab oil became available. While they thought that they could afford to neglect the exploitation of their coal reserves, the nations of Eastern Europe and Far East Asia continued to use coal as their major primary energy resource (see Fig. III C–2).

(D) BRIEF ON AGE STRUCTURE AND POPULATION GROWTH

There are several ways to measure and describe population development. One of the simplest methods for determining population growth consists in counting annually all births and deaths in a country or region, and referring these figures to the number of people living in the considered area at a certain date each year. One thus obtains the so-called crude birth and crude death rates, for example forty-two per thousand inhabitants and twenty-two per thousand, respectively. The difference is then the crude growth rate, in our example twenty per thousand, or 2 percent. If the crude growth rate stays constant, the population grows "exponentially," just as capital grows in a bank with constant compounded interest. The famous "rule of seventy" permits one quickly to determine the number of years after which the population has grown to double its size at a constant growth rate. For our example, of an annual 2 percent growth rate, the rule of seventy would yield $70/2 = 35$ years as the time in which the population doubles. This rule yields sufficiently accurate results for growth rates up to 10 percent.

As "crude growth rate" implies, its application yields only a "crude" approach to the problem of population growth which becomes quite unreliable in the long run, as soon as growth rates fall below 1 percent. This discrepancy results from the fact that there is a close relationship between population growth and age structure and that for low growth rates the age structure of the population changes appreciably in time.

For example, in Fig. III D–1 we have depicted the age structure change for the population of Eastern Europe including the Soviet Union, whose annual growth rate had dropped below 1 percent by 1970. Contrast this with the age structure change, shown in Fig. III D–2, of the fast-increasing population in Latin America (growth rate about 3 percent).

Fertility and mortality were kept constant after 1970. Whereas the age structure changes drastically in Eastern Europe, hardly any change takes place after 1975 in Latin America with its large percentage of children and young people.

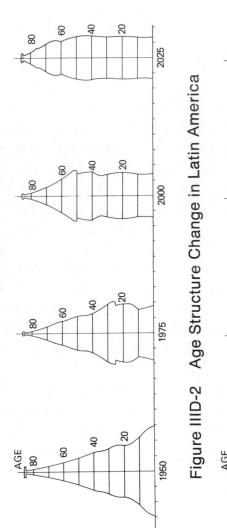

Figure IIID-1 Age Structure Change in Eastern Europe

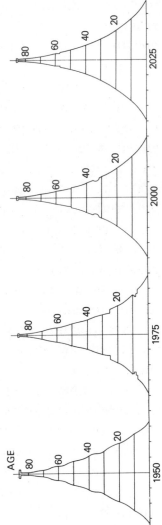

Figure IIID-2 Age Structure Change in Latin America

The number of births obviously depends on the fertility of the female population, and just as obviously, the probability that a woman will give birth depends on her age. Certainly, below the age of fifteen or over age fifty the probability of her giving birth is very small. In Fig. III D–3 the fertility pattern, which proves to be rather stable for certain cultures, has been depicted for two regions, (a) North America, and (b) North Africa and the Middle East. One readily recognizes that in North America the overwhelming majority of children are borne by women between twenty and thirty years of age, after which the probability of their having children decreases rapidly, while in North Africa and the Middle East the span of years during which a woman is likely to bear children is greatly extended. Hence it is no wonder that population growth is far higher there than in North America.

Mortality also plays a big role in determining population growth. Without doubt the increase in the number of people living in the developing countries results from the fact that mortality has decreased greatly in the past thirty years. Population growth would even be much faster than it is if mortality decreased to the level prevailing in the industrialized countries. As Fig. III D–4 shows, mortality (the probability of a person's dying at a certain age) increases rapidly in North America (a) only for groups over seventy years old, while in Main Africa (b) the likelihood of death for infants, children, and younger people is vastly greater than in North America and in the other developed regions.

Let us now assume that fertility and mortality patterns, like those shown here, continue to persist as they have since the end of World War II. As growth rates become smaller, the magnitude of fertility is implicitly reduced compared

Figure IIID-3   Fertility Pattern: (A) North America; (B) North Africa and Middle East

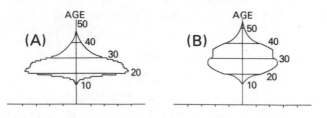

Figure IIID-4   Mortality Pattern: (A) North America; (B) Main Africa

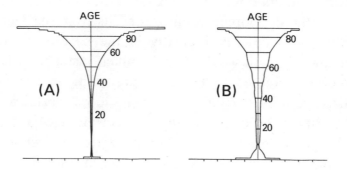

to that of mortality, while the shape of the fertility and mortality diagrams (see Figs. III D–3 and III D–4) remain unchanged. This causes the child base of the age structure to narrow and in time will lead to diminishing the number of women of childbearing age.

Thus, even if fertility were to remain constant, corresponding to, say, the birth rates of 1970, the birth rate would decline appreciably, once it had dropped below, say 2 percent, because the child base of the age structure would become smaller, and after a delay of about twenty years the number of childbearing women would decrease considerably as compared with the rest of the population; at the same time the share of the older people rises at the expense of the young age groups. This causes, even for constant mortality, the death rates to rise because the old age population, for which the probability of dying is greater, has now grown more strongly than the younger age group (see Fig. III D–1).

Fig. III D–5 depicts the future population development in Region 5 (Eastern Europe including the Soviet Union), if present fertility and mortality rates persist. Here the growth rate in 1970 was about 0.7 percent. The rule of seventy would then indicate that with constant birth and death rates the population would double in one hundred years, that is, in 2070 it would have grown to 750 million. But birth and death rates would not stay constant if fertility (age pattern and magnitude) as well as mortality (age pattern and magnitude) were to remain constant. Both the latter parameters are measures more basic than "crude" birth and death rates, which are derived from them, which is why for constant fertility and mortality, corresponding exactly to the crude birth and death rates, respectively, of

Figure IIID-5 Population Development in Eastern Europe (Constant Fertility and Mortality)

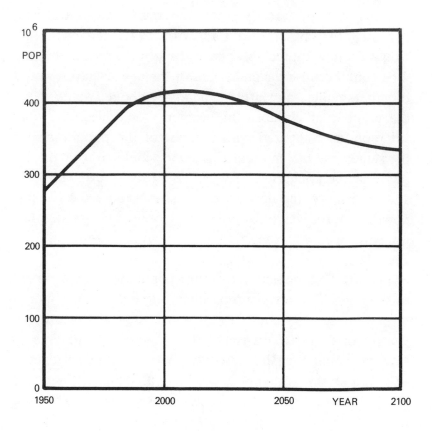

1970, no exponential growth and no population doubling in 2070 takes place. Rather there is first a much slower growth and then after the turn of the century a steady decline due to an underlying pattern of the age structure that becomes increasingly top-heavy (see Fig. III D–1).

In contrast to this behavior we find that in regions with high growth rates, constant fertility also implies practically constant crude birth rate, and constant mortality implies practically constant crude death rate, because the age structure hardly changes over the years (see Fig. III D–2). Therefore in these fast-growing populations constant fertility and mortality lead to exponential growth which eventually has to be stopped because, for example, a sustained 3 percent growth of the Latin American population (presently about 300 million) would by the year 2100 yield about 10 billion inhabitants in Latin America, two and a half times the present total world population.

Hence the question arises as to what change the magnitude of fertility would have to undergo in the various world regions in order to lead to population equilibrium. This is not difficult to calculate, if one assumes that the fertility pattern remains unchanged in addition to constant mortality (pattern and magnitude). Of course, it would also not cause extraordinary difficulties to assume such changes of patterns, but we have not yet done this since we have reason to believe that if an equilibrium policy is initiated within the next decade, the difference would not be considerable.

As Fig. III D–6 shows, in the course of a population equilibrium policy the age structure changes to a certain type, regardless whether the equilibrium policy is applied (a) to an initially fast-growing population of a developing region (Latin America), or (b) to a population in the indus-

Figure IIID-6   Age Structure Development Under Equilibrium Policy: (A) Latin America; (B) North America

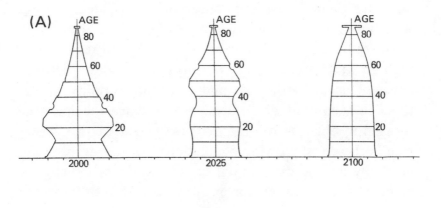

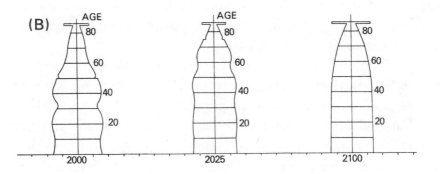

trialized countries with small growth rates (North America). In the end all age structures have the typical bottle shape. It is quite obvious that a population with an age structure that already has certain features of an equilibrium age structure rises only a little more after it has initiated a population equilibrium policy. On the other hand, regions with a pyramidic age structure resting on a very wide base of infants and young children will still experience a large increase in population even after it has initiated its equilibrium policy, because it takes a long time before its age structure has changed into the bottle shape equilibrium age structure (see Fig. III D–6).

For the ten world regions of our model the results of an equilibrium policy initiated at different times with a transition period of thirty-five years are depicted in Fig. III D–7.

Finally, it is interesting to note the relative interregional population change that takes place, if fertility and mortality remain constant after 1970 (Fig. III D–8), or if in all ten regions equilibrium policies are implemented in 1975 (Fig. III D–9). Whereas in the first case—however unlikely—the share of the industrialized regions 1–5 (the "North") drops from 34 percent in 1950 to below 5 percent of the total world population in the year 2100 (see Fig. III D–8), their portion drops in the case of Fig. III D–9 only to little below 25 percent.

Figure IIID-7 Population Growth for All Regions Under Equilibrium Policy

FERTILITY TRANSITION PERIOD 35 YEARS

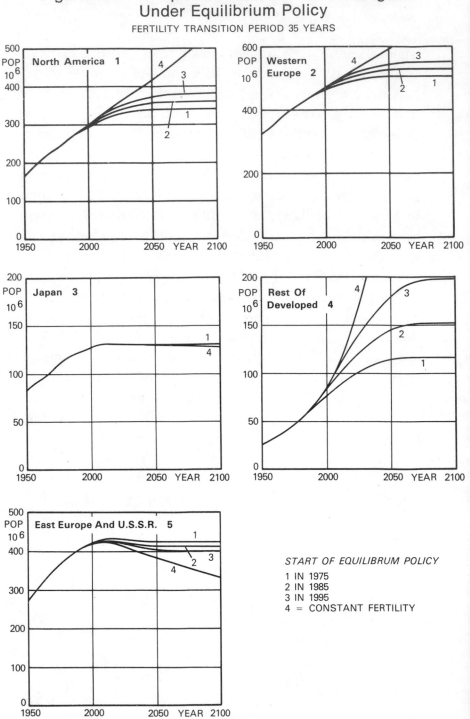

START OF EQUILIBRUM POLICY

1 IN 1975
2 IN 1985
3 IN 1995
4 = CONSTANT FERTILITY

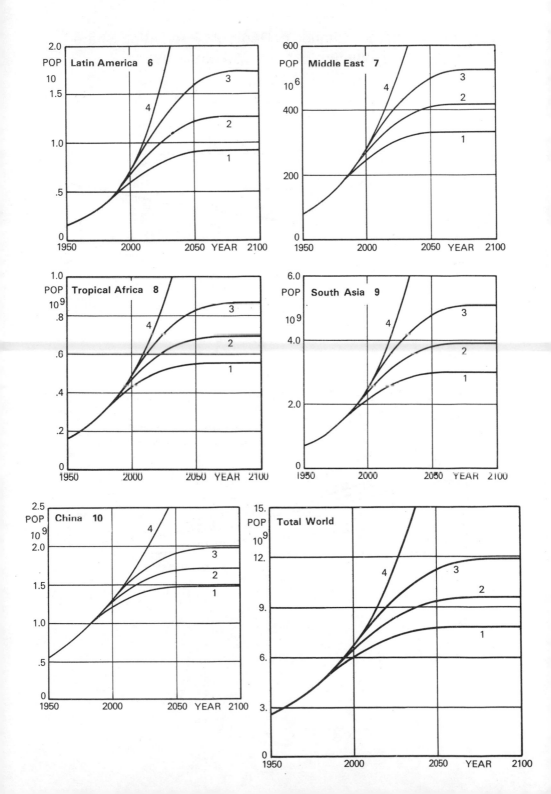

Figure IIID-8 Change of Regional Population Share
(Constant Fertility and Mortality)

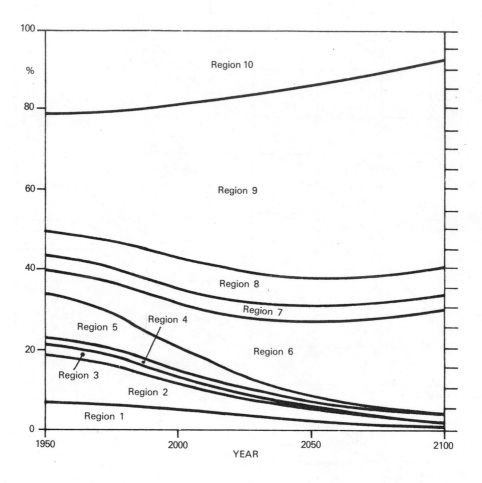

Figure IIID-9 Change of Regional Population Share
(Equilibrium Policy Initiated in 1975)

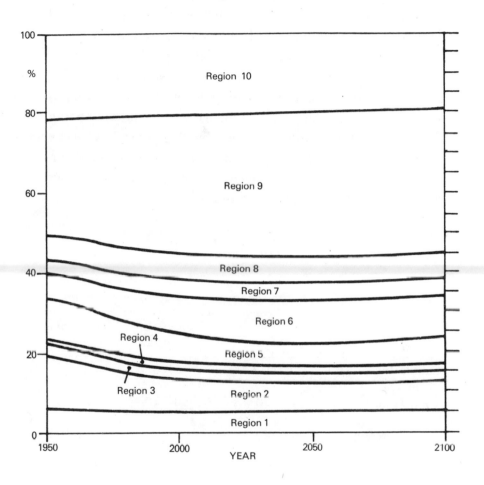

(E) BRIEF ON STARVATION AND MORTALITY

The relationship between nutrition and human health is a complicated subject with many unanswered questions. Certain things, however, are relatively clear. There is little disagreement that the two most significant indicators are calories (energy) and protein. Sufficient quantities of both are vitally important to health and well-being. The table below, based on work by Professor Pokrovsky, Director of the Institute of Nutrition of the Soviet Academy of Science, gives an overview of the great nutrition gap between the industrialized and the developing countries.

TABLE III E–1

	Daily Needs per capita	*Actual Average Daily Consumption per capita*	
		Industrial Countries	*Developing Countries*
Caloric Intake (in Kcal)	2200–3000	3100	2150
Total Protein (in Grams)	70	90–110	35–60
Animal Protein (in Grams)	40	30–70	5–10

This table shows clearly that it is especially the protein supply that is extremely critical in the developing countries. Sufficient calories and insufficient protein in the diet of young children lead to kwashiorkor, which has been recognized as a significant cause of their morbidity and mortality. Protein is life's most important building material. Much of the body's musculoskeletal and vegetative systems are composed largely of protein, as are the enzymes controlling the biochemical metabolic processes. The protein in the body is never in a static state, but is always catabolized (broken down) and renewed. This constant turnover, plus the requirements for growth in children, as well as the lack of any specific storage mechanism for protein in the body, necessitates the daily intake of an adequate amount of protein to prevent an actual net loss of body protein (loss of body tissue). In adults prolonged inadequate protein intake (depending on its severity) causes loss of body substance, increased susceptibility to stress and infection, and ultimately death. We know now that a child, which as a fetus and during its first year of life did not receive sufficient protein, will most probably remain subnormal for life in its mental and physical capacities. The development of the brain and of the central nervous system requires high-quality protein that only animals can provide in the form of milk, eggs, and meat, at least as a substantial addition to vegetable proteins. There are, however, some Asian and African countries where the average daily per-capita intake of animal protein is below 5 grams; this comes as no surprise when we realize that the average citizen of India can spend only ten to fifteen American cents for his daily food.

The present mortality pattern in South Asia as well as elsewhere is certainly conditioned by many factors, including nutrition. Since our model calculations indicate that food per-capita in South Asia will be the factor most likely to undergo the biggest change during the coming decades, we took the deviation from the present per-capita food supply as the determining factor for the relative change in mortality. According to the Technical Report No. 522 of the World Health Organization (WHO, 1973) the age-specific mortality factors affect infants a little more strongly in the case of protein deficiency than in the case of calorie deficiency; therefore we determined an age-specific mortality multiplier as a nonlinear function of relative protein deficiency. We believed that as far as South Asia is concerned, no special consideration of the calorie deficiency was necessary; in this region protein and calorie intake go together, because the diet there contains very little animal protein, the meat consumption being just 3 to 4 percent of that in the United States. For this reason, even if a protein deficiency could be covered, for example, by the addition of synthetic lysine to wheat, the calorie deficiency would remain. It should be noted in this connection that the Indian agricultural expert, P. V. Sukhatme, recently questioned the usefulness of this method of protein enrichment in his presidential address on "Protein Strategy: An Agricultural Development" (*Journal of Agricultural Economics,* XXVII, 1972).

APPENDIX IV

Bibliography of Scientific Papers and Technical Reports

Reports in the Proceedings of the Seminar on the Regionalized Multilevel World Model at the International Institute for Applied Systems Analysis, Laxenburg, Austria, April 29–May 3, 1974.*
Available upon request from the IIASA.

Title	Author
METHODOLOGY	
1) Objectives, Motivation, and Conceptual Foundations	M. Mesarovic, E. Pestel
2) A Goal-Seeking and Regionalized Model for Analysis of Critical World Relationships—The Conceptual Foundation, *Kybernetes Journal,* 1972	M. Mesarovic, E. Pestel
3) Interactive Mode Analysis of En-	B. Hughes, P. Gille, A. Erdilek, C. Loxley,

---

* No further bibliography is given, since all references to other relevant literature can be found in our reports.

Title	Authors
ergy Crisis Using Multilevel World Model; *Futures*, August 1973	R. Pestel, T. Shook, M. Mesarovic
4) Simulation of Value-Controlled Decision-Making: Approach and Prototype	H. Bossel, B. Hughes
5) Human Computer Decision-Making: Notes concerning the Interactive Mode	J. H. G. Klabbers
6) Coordination Principles for System Interactions	Y. Takahara
7) Conversational Use of Multi-Layer Decision Models	F. Rechenmann
8) PROMETHEE (Programmed support for Models of Earth Trends, Hierarchical, Economic, Ecologic)	J. Mermet

POPULATION

9) Population Model, Vols. I and II	K. H. Oehmen, W. Paul

ECONOMICS

10) Methodology for Construction of World Economic Model	M. Mesarovic, E. Pestel
11) Specification of Structure for a Macro-Economic World Model	B. Hickman, L. Klein, M. Mesarovic
12) Computer Implementation of Macro-Economic World Model	P. Gille, K. Kominek, R. Pestel, T. Shook, W. Stroebele
13) Implementation of Micro-Economic Model	T. Shook
14) Cobb-Douglas Production Function for the World Model Project and a One-Sector Growth Model Interpretation	M. McCarthy, G. Shuttic
15) Statistical Analysis of Error Propagation in World Economic Model	G. Blankenship

Title	Authors

ENERGY

16) Energy Model: Resources   R. Bauerschmidt, R. Denton, H.-H. Maier

17) Energy Model: Demand   B. Hughes, N. Chu

18) Energy Model: Supply   H. Bossel

19) Regionalized World Liquid Fuels Production and Consumption from 1925–1965   N. Chu

20) A Description of the World Oil Model   B. Hughes

21) Assessment of the World Oil Crisis Using the Multilevel World Model   B. Hughes, M. Mesarovic, E. Pestel

22) Global Energy Model   R. P. Heyes, R. A. Jerdonek, A. B. Kuper

23) Environmental Impact Assessment   M. Gottwald, R. Pestel

FOOD

24) A Regionalized Food Model for the Global System   W. B. Clapham, Jr., M. Warshaw, T. Shook

25) The Integrated Food Policy Analysis Model: Structural Description and Sensitivity Analysis   M. Mesarovic, J. M. Richardson, Jr., M. Warshaw

26) Scenario Analysis of the World Food Problem, 1974–2025, Using the Integrated Food Policy Analysis Model   W. B. Clapham, Jr., M. Mesarovic, T. Shook J. M. Richardson, Jr., M. Warshaw, T. Shook

27) A Model for the Relationship between Selected Nutritional Variables and Excess Mortality in Populations   T. Weisman

WATER RESOURCES

28) Water Resources Model   M. Cardenas

COMMENTARY

We most warmly welcome this report by Mihajlo Mesarovic and Eduard Pestel to The Club of Rome. It marks an important new step toward understanding the global natural and human systems within which we live. And it appears as a book for wide distribution at an opportune time. Under the impact of worsening world situations, public opinion has greatly matured in the last few years. However, decision-makers in every country and the world establishment generally, although forced to face up to the stark realities of our age, are still reluctant to renovate their thinking and modes of action. The Mesarovic-Pestel work will confront them with a compelling frame of references that can hardly be ignored, offering them at the same time a new, potentially powerful tool to test out the validity or futility of their views and their policies in the real world framework.

The need for clear understanding of the working of the global systems and the organic interdependence of their parts is at the very heart of the concern of The Club of Rome. When, in 1968, we began to discuss these matters, we were deeply impressed by the unexplored interactions between the major problems besetting human society and by the fact that in nearly all policy formulation and administrative action such interactions are largely ignored. Of course, philosophers have, from ancient times, stressed the unity of existence and the interconnection of all the elements of nature, man and thought. However, their teaching has seldom been reflected in political or social behavior.

The very principles of the sovereign national state, the structures and procedures of government, and the dispersion and linear nature of their policies are ill-adapted to the practical acceptance of these kinds of concepts. In the past, the consequences of any such discordance, even when profound, could eventually be remedied by action "after the dust is settled." Today, with the inescapable influence of scale, of complexity, and of rapid rates of change, we no longer have such periods of grace, while the penalties we must pay for disregarding the cross impacts of problems and attempted solutions or indulging in conflicting national or regional goals are becoming ever more severe. At this point, it is impossible to set mankind on a safe course again unless the ensuing stream of crises is stopped and the still graver crises ahead are prevented.

The Club of Rome's first attempt at understanding the unprecedented tangle called "the world problematique" was made by sponsoring a world simulation model realized with the system dynamics technique of Professor Jay Forrester of MIT and culminated in the well-known study published in 1972 under the title *The Limits to Growth*. In it, Professor

Dennis Meadows and his team projected into the future a number of interacting critical phenomena with a view to indicating what might happen to the world systems if present trends were allowed to continue.

The conclusions of this first global research were generally taken to be a prophecy of doom, despite the repeated statements of the book itself that the purpose of the project was indeed to elucidate the consequences of continuing as at present in order to provoke change which would render these conclusions invalid. The energy and food crises exploded in the meantime with such vicious force that they cut short much of the hasty criticism leveled against this exercise. While readily recognizing the inevitable imperfections of the MIT pioneering effort, we regard it as a milestone; not the least significant result is that world attention has begun to consider seriously the basic issues raised by that report.

Now Mesarovic and Pestel have taken a completely new point of departure. One of the deliberate limitations of the previous research was its adoption of worldwide aggregations. This was a matter of choice, prompted by the objective of completing the project rapidly, providing at the same time an initial overall perspective of the trends and constraints inherent in the dynamics of the total system. We knew, of course, that the heterogeneity of the world, with its innumerable cultural and environmental differences, varying levels of development and uneven distribution of natural resources, means the consequences of growth in different places is likewise heterogeneous. Thus the *average* curves and trends, as outlined in the first report, could not be adopted as a guide to detailed policy decisions in any particular country.

We appreciated therefore the urgent need to follow up

this initial global model with disaggregated studies that could lead to a deeper understanding of the wide range of world, regional and national prospects and to their being coupled with the practical business of politics. And, consequently, we supported the Mesarovic-Pestel study which aims to do just this. Their world model, based on new developments of the multilevel hierarchical systems theory, divides the world into ten interdependent and mutually interacting regions of political, economic or environmental coherence, and is capable of breaking down its data into still smaller units, such as that of the single nation, if necessary. This means that its findings can be relevant to national policy-makers. Moreover, for the first time it is now possible, by confronting the policies of different groups competing among themselves within the finite capacity of the planet, to delineate areas of conflict or incompatibility inherent in national or regional policies.

The difficult task of decision-making is normally an uncertain art. Objectives may be more or less clearly defined, political or ideological principles may offer sound guidelines, and even good statistical data and qualitative analyses of the given situation may be available; but the process—the desired option—is less clear, often less rational. Decisions are usually based on the human assessment of these and many other factors and on accumulated experience as to the probable consequence of particular actions. The normal, mental model of the decision-maker is relatively simple. An individual may have great qualities of intuition and a fine sense of political, social and psychological reality, but man is unable to assimilate and interact multiple variables with any certainty.

What the computerized model can offer is the reinforcement of human qualities with an input of analyzed data, thus making possible the exploration of alternatives. For some people this approach is a technocratic menace: the computer taking over responsibility for human destiny. This is nonsense; particularly in the case of the Mesarovic-Pestel work. Their methodology is very promising and flexible as it allows for a continuous dialogue between man, who retains his value system, judgment and purpose, and computer, which puts at his disposal its enormous calculation capacity. Human initiative or human response to stress and challenge is not only maintained in a dominant position, but strengthened by an appropriate aid that allows one to study alternative scenarios, test out various options by assessment of their probable consequences, and finally upgrade and rationalize policy decisions.

Criticism was often made of *The Limits to Growth* in that it was concerned exclusively with material limits—which are never likely to be reached, since political and other difficulties will precede them. No doubt, the real limits to growth are social, political and managerial, and finally reside within the nature of man. In the Meadows model it was not easy to relate directly material problems with the political process or with changes in the value system. New tools were indeed necessary to allow for an organic socio-political-economic coupling. One is now presented to us by Mesarovic-Pestel.

In carrying out this work, they have aspired, in the tradition of The Club of Rome, to be non-partisan in current political terms. The chief problems of the world today are not essentially problems of party politics and, being relevant to the very survival of man, they even transcend current ideologies. Of course, complete objectivity is impossible, however earnestly it may be sought. Bias is unconsciously and subtly built in through the selection of data and assumptions which reflect the views and conditioning of those who select them. In the present instance, for example, a general long-term solution of mankind's energy problem by the use of nuclear power, particularly through the use of fast-breeder reactors, is rejected. The authors, turning away from the Faustian bargain, opt for solar energy, although presumably the door is open for nuclear fusion if that becomes available in time. We fully agree with this rejection, but it is a value judgment nevertheless.

It will be recognized of course that these are still prototype models. Mesarovic and Pestel have assumed a herculean task. The full implementation of their work will take many years of trial and error and intellectual ingenuity, and will in the end require a comprehensive bank of coherent world, regional and national data if it is to have sufficient flexibility to allow the switching in and out of large numbers of relevant variables, the continuous reappraisal of data and assumptions, and the exploration of the effect that changes in the system of values would have.

Results to date, however, are already very important. The authors have concentrated on several clusters of problems which, if not squarely met, can, alone, provoke unimaginable disasters. Backed by this intensive research and study, certain basic conclusions have been reached. They confirm earlier warnings of The Club of Rome. Two of them should be quoted here:

> No fundamental redressment of the world conditions and human prospects is possible except by worldwide cooperation in a global context and with long views.

> The cost, not only in economic and political terms,

but in human suffering as well, which will result from
delay in taking early decisions, are simply monstrous.

The reader of this book has certainly found that these
conclusions and many corollary ones are buttressed by a
thesis whose detail may be disputed, but whose general sense
is, in our view, abundantly convincing. The question is
whether these warnings will be heeded. In the past, no
human group has been able to formulate long-term policies
in the interest of mankind, and today policy delays mar the
management of human affairs even when minor interests
are in conflict.

This book helps us realize that we are on a fatal course.
How can a true world community emerge, or even our
present human society survive when it is ridden by profound
and intolerable injustices, overpopulation and megafamines,
while it is crippled by energy and materials shortages, and
eaten up by inflation? What explosions or breakdowns will
occur, and where and when, now that nuclear war technology and civil violence are outrunning the pace of political wisdom and stability?

The odds seem against man. Yet we are moderately
hopeful. The winds of change have begun to blow. A keen
and anxious awareness is evolving to suggest that fundamental changes will have to take place in the world order
and its power structures, in the distribution of wealth and
income, in our own outlook and behavior. Perhaps only a
new and enlightened humanism can permit mankind to
negotiate this transition without irreparable lacerations.

In the UN, for example, new concepts such as that of
"world collective economic security" as a necessary correla-
tive to political security, and an innovative "charter of du-

ties and rights" of member states is under consideration. In April 1974, a special session of the Assembly issued a declaration on the establishment of a "new international economic order." And the UN world conferences—first on man and his environment, followed by studies on population, food, and the law of the seas, with planned sessions on energy and materials, human settlements, etc.—address themselves to global problems and global solutions.

These are the ferments of an inevitable revolution in international relations; they herald a different management of the human society. Last February in Salzburg The Club of Rome convened a meeting of senior statesmen from different countries and cultures to discuss global problems and long-term alternatives for human society. The concluding statement interpreted the meeting as unequivocally indicating that "a new spirit of active solidarity and cooperation" among all peoples and nations—called the *Spirit of Salzburg* —is indispensable for mankind to face the challenge of our time.

Many of the decisions for survival which must be taken in this spirit will inevitably be unpopular and some impossible to achieve, unless there is universal understanding of the nature of our problems and their gravity. The importance of this book is manifest under both these aspects. On the one hand, it explicitly lays bare the alternatives ahead, showing the urgency of making responsible choices. On the other hand, it has developed a learning and operative instrument which can assist us in making these choices.

It is for these reasons that we recommend this report to the political class and to the public. At the same time, we express the hope that resources be made available to develop further these techniques so that those of us who have the tremendous responsibility of making major decisions at this turn of history be aided to make them in the true interest of the peoples of the world, today and tomorrow.

Aurelio Peccei
Alexander King

July 1974

INDEX OF BRIEFS AND FIGURES

209